BARRON'S B

BY

Margaret A. Robinson
Lecturer
Widener University

SERIES EDITOR

Michael Spring
Editor, *Literary Cavalcade*
Scholastic Inc.

BARRON'S

BARRON'S EDUCATIONAL SERIES, INC.

ACKNOWLEDGMENTS

We would like to acknowledge the many painstaking hours of work Holly Hughes and Thomas F. Hirsch have devoted to making the *Book Notes* series a success.

All inquiries should be addressed to:
Barron's Educational Series, Inc.
250 Wireless Boulevard
Hauppauge, New York 11788

Library of Congress Catalog Card No. 84-18479

International Standard Book No. 0-8120-3429-5

Library of Congress Cataloging in Publication Data
Robinson, Margaret A.
   Homer's The Odyssey.

   (Barron's book notes)
   Bibliography: p. 84
   Summary: A guide to reading "The Odyssey" with a
critical and appreciative mind encouraging analysis of
plot, style, form, and structure. Also includes background
on the author's life and times, sample tests, term
paper suggestions, and a reading list.
   1. Homer, Odyssey. 2. Odysseus (Greek mythology) in
literature. [1. Homer, Odyssey. 2. Classical literature
—History and criticism] I. Title. II. Series.
PA4167.R65   1984   883'.01   84-18479
ISBN 0-8120-3429-5 (pbk.)

CONTENTS

HOW TO USE THIS BOOK

You have to know how to approach literature in order to get the most out of it. This *Barron's Book Notes* volume follows a plan based on methods used by some of the best students to read a work of literature.

Begin with the guide's section on the author's life and times. As you read, try to form a clear picture of the author's personality, circumstances, and motives for writing the work. This background usually will make it easier for you to hear the author's tone of voice, and follow where the author is heading.

Then go over the rest of the introductory material—such sections as those on the plot, characters, setting, themes, and style of the work. Underline, or write down in your notebook, particular things to watch for, such as contrasts between characters and repeated literary devices. At this point, you may want to develop a system of symbols to use in marking your text as you read. (Of course, you should only mark up a book you own, not one that belongs to another person or a school.) Perhaps you will want to use a different letter for each character's name, a different number for each major theme of the book, a different color for each important symbol or literary device. Be prepared to mark up the pages of your book as you read. Put your marks in the margins so you can find them again easily.

Now comes the moment you've been waiting for—the time to start reading the work of literature. You may want to put aside your *Barron's Book Notes* volume until you've read the work all the way through. Or you may want to alternate, reading the *Book Notes* analysis of each section as soon as you have finished reading the corresponding part of the original. Before you move on, reread crucial passages you don't fully understand. (Don't take this guide's analysis for granted—make up your own mind as to what the work means.)

Once you've finished the whole work of literature, you may want to review it right away, so you can firm up your ideas about what it means. You may want to leaf through the book concentrating on passages you marked in reference to one character or one theme. This is also a good time to reread the *Book Notes* introductory material, which pulls together insights on specific topics.

When it comes time to prepare for a test or to write a paper, you'll already have formed ideas about the work. You'll be able to go back through it, refreshing your memory as to the author's exact words and perspective, so that you can support your opinions with evidence drawn straight from the work. Patterns will emerge, and ideas will fall into place; your essay question or term paper will almost write itself. Give yourself a dry run with one of the sample tests in the guide. These tests present both multiple-choice and essay questions. An accompanying section gives answers to the multiple-choice questions as well as suggestions for writing the essays. If you have to select a term paper topic, you may choose one from the list of suggestions in this book. This guide also provides you with a reading list, to help you when you start research for a term paper, and a selection of provocative comments by critics, to spark your thinking before you write.

THE AUTHOR AND HIS TIMES

Authorship of *The Odyssey* is attributed to a person called Homer. Not much is known about him. Some scholars believe there were two Homers, one who composed *The Iliad* and another who composed its sequel, *The Odyssey*. It has even been suggested— sometimes playfully, sometimes seriously—that Homer was a woman.

The general view is that Homer was the last in a long line of poet-performers who recited or chanted or sang stories of the heroic past. He was from the Ionian area of Greece. He probably couldn't read or write. *The Iliad* and *The Odyssey* reached their highest form through his telling of them. He used familiar material that had been passed along through the ages by word of mouth, but he shaped this material and embellished it. These two epic poems were probably written down by someone else around 750 B.C., five hundred years after the fall of Troy.

These two stories are all about the Trojan War, the war between the Greeks (Homer calls them the Akhaians) and the Trojans. The quarrel began when Helen, the beautiful wife of king Menelaos, was stolen away to Troy by Paris, the son of Priam, king of Troy. The wronged husband rounded up an army. He got his brother Agamemnon and powerful friends like Akhilleus (Achilles) and Odysseus to do the same. These Greek kings sailed with their troops to Troy, made war on the Trojans, and then laid siege to the walled city of Troy where the Trojans holed up. The siege dragged on, and eventually the war reached a stalemate.

The Greeks were about to give up when Odysseus had them build an enormous hollow horse, fill it with soldiers sworn to silence, and leave it outside the city walls, apparently as a parting tribute to the might of the Trojans. When the Greeks had sailed out of sight, the Trojans brought the horse into the city. Under cover of darkness, the soldiers emerged from the horse, attacked the city, and opened the gates to their comrades who had sailed back to shore. Troy fell. All of these events are said to have taken ten years. *The Iliad* (the Greek word for Troy is *Ilium*) focuses on the two best fighters in the war: Akhilleus, representing the Greeks, and Hector, the hero of the Trojans. *The Odyssey* is about the adventures of Odysseus on his way home from the war.

The gods of the Greek civilization are important in the stories. These gods behave like the kings and queens in *The Iliad* and *The Odyssey*. They have human form and very human behavior; they fall in and out of love, are jealous, cruel, angry, vain, and manipulative. But they're one step higher than even the highest Greeks because they're immortal, and they demand from the race of men a certain respect.

Odysseus is admired by the gods for his coolness under pressure, his quick and convincing lies, his detachment, and his persistence. But men can go too far, and the gods are severe in punishing *hubris* (arrogance) or neglect of respectful rituals. Similarly, among mortals the worst crime is lack of loyalty. Loyalty, wisdom, hospitality, and friendship are high ideals for the Akhaians.

The singer-poets are thought to have accompanied themselves on a simple instrument made of strings pulled taut over some sort of resonator, perhaps a tortoise shell. This instrument was strummed for an occasional rhythmic accent. Since they were reciting and improvising, they made use of "epithets," descriptive tags to fill out a line of verse as well as provide detail about character. Thus, Homer called Odysseus the "raider of cities," and Menelaos is referred to as "the red-haired captain."

The singer-poets also used set pieces such as some of the repeated stories and long comparisons—epic similes—you will find in the poem. These epithets, repeated stories, and epic similes gave the singer-poet a breather. A jazz musician repeats familiar phrases between improvisations. A practiced public speaker uses some tried and true anecdotes. Similarly, Homer's poem is a mix of fresh and standard material.

When *The Odyssey* was finally recorded it was written by hand on a scroll, probably made of papyrus reed. From the original, copies were made, first on papyrus, later on vellum, which was animal skin specially prepared for writing. Neither of these materials lasts forever, and what gets copied and preserved is a matter of changing taste. But Homer was a champion in the struggle for literary survival. When scholars took stock of surviving Egyptian papyri in 1963 they found that nearly half of the 1,596 individual "books" were copies of *The Iliad* or *The Odyssey* or comments about them. During the Classic Age of Greece—the time of the playwright Sophocles and the philosopher Plato—if a Greek owned any books at all, they were likely to be a papyrus scroll of *The Iliad* or *The Odyssey*. He would also probably have memorized long stretches of the two poems. Even today *The Odyssey* is more widely read than any other classic of Greek literature. The ocean spray, the exotic islands, and the story's adventures are infectious. People have even boarded ships and tried to retrace Odysseus' journey, book in hand.

New translations keep coming along. There are more than thirty to choose from in English alone. Some translations, like the popular one by W. H. D. Rouse, are in prose, which some readers may prefer. This guide is based on Robert Fitzgerald's translation because it, like the original, is in verse, and also because its language is easy and down to earth. Since references to the twenty-four books that made up the story are standard, this guide can be used with any translation.

You will find some variation in the English spellings of the Greek names in *The Odyssey*. Fitzgerald uses a *k* instead of a *c* to emphasize the hard sounds of Kirke (Circe), Kyklopes (Cyclops), Klytaimnestra (Clytemnestra), and Akhaians (Acheans). Fitzgerald gives a guide to pronunciation by using stress marks, which helps you hear that, for instance, *Penélopê* rhymes with *catástrophê*, not with *cántaloupe*. Fitzgerald says *The Odyssey* can no more be translated into English than rhododendron can be translated into dogwood—that really to experience Homer a person must learn Greek. Fortunately he went ahead and translated it anyway. His *Odyssey* is full of life—it is a terrific story.

THE POEM

The Plot

Homer doesn't begin his story at the beginning and go straight through to the end. Instead he starts in medias res, in the middle of things. He was elaborating on a story familiar to his listeners, so he didn't have to worry about confusing them. He could build some anticipation in his audience by telling them about his hero before actually bringing Odysseus on stage. He could remind his listeners that men are less important than gods by beginning with the gods.

The gods on Mount Olympos are discussing the fate of Odysseus. For eight years he has been detained on Ogygia, Kalypso's island. Athena, his patron among the gods, thinks it is time for them to help Odysseus to return home. Zeus, the most powerful of the gods, explains that Odysseus offended Poseidon, the god of the sea, by blinding his son, the Kyklopes. In anger Poseidon had sent storms to blow Odysseus' ships off course. But Zeus agrees with Athena that it's now high time that Odysseus be allowed to try again to reach home, and Zeus sends a message to Kalypso to that effect.

In the meantime, Athena goes to Ithaka. She advises Odysseus' son Telemakhos to call an assembly to try to get community support in opposing Penelope's suitors. (Penelope is Odysseus' wife. During her husband's long absence a number of men have·been trying to gain her affections.) He should also set sail in search of news of his father.

NOTE: As you can already see, *The Odyssey* is not
a single story; there are many subplots. You may be
confused at this point. How can Penelope be considering remarriage? Her husband isn't dead. And why
is Odysseus' son Telemakhos looking for him? You
know where he is. You know all these things because
you have been able to listen to the gods' conversation.
But all Penelope and Telemakhos know is that Odysseus left twenty years ago to fight in the Trojan War.
They haven't seen or heard from him since.

Telemakhos calls a meeting of the assembly but gets
no help with his problem. The suitors claim that
Penelope should settle matters herself by remarrying.
With Athena's help he finds a crew and a ship and
departs.

First Telemakhos visits Nestor, who was at Troy
and knows Odysseus well. There is much feasting
and storytelling, but Telemakhos gets no hard news
about Odysseus. He travels overland to see another of
his father's old army buddies, Menelaos. More feasting. Helen, Menelaos' wife, tells stories of the siege of
Troy. Menelaos was detained on the way home
because he had offended Zeus. He wrestled the seer,
Proteus, and defeated him. So Proteus had to tell
Menelaos the truth. He told Menelaos about Odysseus' situation with Kalypso. Meanwhile, the suitors
plot to ambush Telemakhos on his return.

Hermes arrives at Ogygia with the message from
Zeus to release Odysseus. Kalypso agrees. Odysseus
builds a ship and sets sail, but is soon shipwrecked by
Poseidon. (Apparently Poseidon doesn't feel that
eight years in exile is sufficient revenge.) Odysseus
swims to Skheria, home of King Alkinoos.

Odysseus does not at first reveal his identity but King Alkinoos makes this stranger welcome. Feasting and games. A bard sings heroic legends of Troy, which make Odysseus weep, because he was there.

Odysseus then tells who he is, and begins the tale of how he got to Skheria. He relates how he left Troy, fought at the island of Ismaros, and saw the sleepy life of the Lotos Eaters. He blinded and tricked the one-eyed cannibal, Kyklopes, the son of Poseidon. Odysseus acquired a bag of storm winds at Aiolia, was attacked by the Laistrygonians, and had his men bewitched by Kirke. He buried Elpenor, one of his crewmembers who was killed during all this carrying on.

Then Odysseus resisted the song of the Seirenes, and sailed between the whirlpool and the cliff, personified by the names of Skylla and Kharybdis. But his men made the mistake of eating the forbidden cattle of the sun god, Helios. So Zeus wrecked Odysseus' ship, drowning all his men. Odysseus managed to survive Skylla and Kharybdis again, and washed up at Ogygia Island where he stayed eight years with Kalypso. Just recently, he was able to build a ship and set out again for Ithaka, but he was shipwrecked by Poseidon and swam to Skheria, where Nausikaa, King Alkinoos' daughter, found him.

Now that Homer has brought us up to date, the remainder of the story is told straightforwardly in chronological order.

Odysseus is returned safely to Ithaka by the people of Skheria. Athena warns him of the disorder surrounding Penelope at his home, and she disguises him as an elderly beggar. She tells him that she has sent Telemakhos off to seek news and to make his name, but now she will bring him home. She knows of the plot to ambush Odysseus, and will foil it.

Odysseus, in his disguise, meets the swineherd Eumaios, and tests his loyalty with a false story. Eumaios gives Odysseus his cloak, a sign of his piety and hospitality toward strangers. He is also loyal; he has been waiting twenty years for his master to return.

On instructions from Athena, Telemakhos leaves Menelaos and returns safely to Ithaka. Telemakhos goes to Eumaios' hut and offers hospitality and gifts to the disguised Odysseus. Telemakhos sends Eumaios to tell Penelope of his safe arrival. Father and son are reunited when Odysseus reveals his identity.

Still disguised, Odysseus enters his own home. His faithful old dog recognizes him and then dies. The chief suitor, Antinoos, insults Odysseus by throwing a stool at him. The suitors make Odysseus fight a real beggar for their amusement. Odysseus wins, but continues to suffer abuse. Omens such as thunder and the flights of birds of prey indicate the gods' anger at the suitors' impious behavior. Justice is about to be done.

Bathing the feet of the "beggar," Eurykleia recognizes Odysseus by a scar, but she remains silent. Penelope tells the disguised Odysseus that her husband was an accomplished archer and had a formidable bow. He could shoot it through the apertures in twelve axes in a row. The suitor who can perform this feat on the following day, will win her. Having made her decision, Penelope despairs. More omens predict doom.

The next day Odysseus reveals his identity to Eumaios. The suitors try to string the bow and fail. Odysseus strings it and shoots through the axes.

The suitors are now trapped defenseless inside the courtyard. A goatherd, Melanthios, climbs the wall and brings them weapons from the storeroom. Athena (disguised) aids in the slaughter of the suitors. Melanthios' disloyalty is punished by torture and mutilation. Twelve corrupt maid servants are hanged. The courtyard is cleansed and purified.

Odysseus is restored to his true form. When Penelope sees him, she is confused and overcome. She tests his identity, saying the master's bed has been moved. Odysseus had built this bed with an olive stump as one bedpost. His anger and his knowledge of the secret of the bed convince Penelope that he is indeed her beloved Odysseus. Husband and wife are reunited.

The dead suitors join the souls in the underworld. Odysseus is reunited with Laertes, his aged father. The relatives of the suitors demand vengeance. Laertes kills the father of Antinoos. The intervention of Athena brings final peace.

Did It Really Happen?

Was there a Troy? Did the grand palaces of the Greeks (the Akhaians) really exist, splendidly decorated in bronze, gold, and ivory? Was there really a man called Odysseus?

It's hard to know for certain. Although the poems were written down about 750 B.C., the events in them probably took place as long ago as 1600 to 1200 B.C. This period is called the Bronze Age because that was when people discovered how to mix tin and copper to make bronze. From this durable yet workable material they crafted impressive artistic objects as well as tools and equipment. Not much is known about this period. But for centuries people have been fascinated by the Bronze Age heroes in Homer's stories, and this fascination has led to much research and investigation.

Three discoveries have convinced scholars of the truth behind the legends. In 1876, Heinrich Schliemann, a retired merchant and amateur archaeologist, unearthed a burial circle at Mycenae on mainland Greece. The gold and bronze materials, and the high degree of artistry in the objects he found, made it clear that an advanced, aristocratic people had lived there, people like the ones Homer described. In 1900, Arthur Evans excavated Knossos on the island of Crete and found more similar treasure, evidently the riches of the powerful King Minos. The name and reputation of Minos, like those of Agamemnon, Menelaos, and Odysseus, had come down through the ages in the oral legends.

The link between myth and legend is very close. For example, the myth of Theseus, Ariadne, and a monster called the Minotaur says that Ariadne helped Theseus through a labyrinth by giving him a spool of thread and a sword. With the sword he could kill the Minotaur, with the thread he could find his way back out. Legend tells that a gift of maidens and youths was sent as a tribute each year to King Minos. It doesn't take much imagination to turn the cruel king into a monster, and his vast, complex palace into a labyrinth. King Minos and Crete dominated mainland Greece until eventually Mycenae superseded the mother city.

In 1952 another gifted amateur, Michael Ventris, who was trained as an architect, not as an archaeologist, deciphered the writing called Linear B found on clay tablets in these two digs. What he was able to read was not Homeric poetry, but merchants' accounts, yet his cracking of the code made it clear that the Minoans and Mycenaeans were Greek and spoke Greek. Of course, the early Akhaian material of these times was altered and expanded over the centuries of oral transmission. But the archaeological evidence gives a basis in fact to Homer's stories.

Around the time of the fall of Troy (roughly 1260 B.C.) the flourishing Greek civilization collapsed under raids by a less-advanced group called the Dorians. Mycenae at its most prosperous was the size of a little country town, and the effect of even these small-scale raids was disastrous, resulting in a Dark Ages from which the Greek peoples took five hundred years to recover. The cities were burned; writing disappeared until around 776 B.C. when the Phoenician alphabet was adopted by the Greeks. It's a tribute to Homer as a poet and to the power of the stories that they survived.

The Characters

Characters in *The Odyssey* do not have last names, but they are often identified in terms of their fathers, such as "Penelope, Ikarios' faithful daughter"; place of residence, such as "Nestor, whose home is sandy Pylos"; and epithets (descriptive tags) such as "lion-hearted Akhilleus."

MAJOR CHARACTERS

Odysseus
The name Odysseus has been translated a number of ways. Odysseus' grandfather, a notorious thief and thus not a popular fellow, gave him the name. It

means "the person people love to hate." Once while telling one of his false stories Odysseus introduces himself as "Quarrelman." One scholar says his name means "trouble," but the usual translation is "Victim of Enmity." The word *odyssey* means the journey of Odysseus, long and full of adventure, rich with people and places, never in a straight line—a life. If you took a couple of months to drive from San Diego to Boston in an unreliable car, breaking down, camping, meeting people, and making side excursions along the way, you could call your trip an odyssey.

Odysseus is an epic hero. He's a legendary figure with more than the usual amount of brains and muscle. Sometimes he's almost superhuman. At the end of the story, with only his inexperienced son and two farmhands to help, he kills more than a hundred of Penelope's suitors. He's able to do it because he has the help of the goddess Athena. He embodies the ideals Homeric Greeks aspired to: manly valor, loyalty, piety, and intelligence. Piety means being respectful of the gods, acknowledging their control of fate, knowing you need their help. Odysseus' intelligence is a mix of keen observation, instinct, and street smarts. He's extremely cautious. He's good at disguises and at concealing his feelings. He's a fast, inventive liar.

Odysseus is also very human, and you get to see him in many roles. He is often moved to tears. He makes mistakes, gets into tricky situations, and loses his temper. You see him as a husband, father, and son. In addition, you see him as an athlete, army captain, sailor, carpenter, storyteller, ragged beggar, lover. He is both brutal and sensitive, bold and shy.

When the Irish writer James Joyce was looking for a universal man as a hero for his book *Ulysses,* he chose Odysseus. (Ulysses is the Latin version of Odysseus.)

od. But for centuries people have been fascinated by the Bronze Age heroes in Homer's stories, and this fascination has led to much research and investigation.

Three discoveries have convinced scholars of the truth behind the legends. In 1876, Heinrich Schliemann, a retired merchant and amateur archaeologist, unearthed a burial circle at Mycenae on mainland Greece. The gold and bronze materials, and the high degree of artistry in the objects he found, made it clear that an advanced, aristocratic people had lived there, people like the ones Homer described. In 1900, Arthur Evans excavated Knossos on the island of Crete and found more similar treasure, evidently the riches of the powerful King Minos. The name and reputation of Minos, like those of Agamemnon, Menelaos, and Odysseus, had come down through the ages in the oral legends.

The link between myth and legend is very close. For example, the myth of Theseus, Ariadne, and a monster called the Minotaur says that Ariadne helped Theseus through a labyrinth by giving him a spool of thread and a sword. With the sword he could kill the Minotaur, with the thread he could find his way back out. Legend tells that a gift of maidens and youths was sent as a tribute each year to King Minos. It doesn't take much imagination to turn the cruel king into a monster, and his vast, complex palace into a labyrinth. King Minos and Crete dominated mainland Greece until eventually Mycenae superseded the mother city.

In 1952 another gifted amateur, Michael Ventris, who was trained as an architect, not as an archaeologist, deciphered the writing called Linear B found on clay tablets in these two digs. What he was able to

read was not Homeric accounts, yet his cracking that the Minoans and Myc spoke Greek. Of course, the these times was altered an turies of oral transmission. dence gives a basis in fact

Around the time of the B.C.) the flourishing Gr under raids by a less-adva ans. Mycenae at its most little country town, and th scale raids was disastrou from which the Greek years to recover. The cit appeared until around 7 alphabet was adopted b Homer as a poet and to they survived.

The C

Characters in The O but they are often ide such as "Penelope, I of residence, such as Pylos"; and epithets hearted Akhilleus."

MAJOI

Odysseus
The name Odyss
of ways. Odysseus'
thus not a popula

means "
telling o
himself a
means "
of Enmit
Odysseu
ple and
took a co
Boston in
meeting
the way,
Odysse
with more
cle. Some
of the stor
farmhands
Penelope's
the help of
als Homeri
piety, and
of the god
knowing y
is a mix o
smarts. He
guises and
inventive lia
Odysseus
him in man
makes mista
his temper.
son. In addit
tain, sailor,
er. He is bot
When the
universal ma
Odysseus. (U

Many people consider *The Odyssey* one of the finest books ever written. This is because Odysseus is such an alive character and, no matter what the century, so much like us.

Telemakhos (Telemachus)

The secondary hero of the story is Odysseus' son, Telemakhos. As the story progresses you learn more and more about Odysseus' character. You see, too, growth and development in his twenty-year-old son. He changes from a passive, untested boy to a young man proudly standing at his father's side. When the relatives of the suitors come for vengeance, he is ready to take them on.

The boy Telemakhos learns to be a man of valor and action. He is respectful to gods and men, and loyal to his mother and father, siding with them against the suitors. He shows intelligence in his behavior with Nestor and Menelaos. But he also exhibits another important Greek ideal: hospitality. Any stranger or beggar coming to the door may be a god in disguise, so such wanderers must be treated well. They are not asked questions until their needs for food, drink, and comfort are met. Telemakhos' open-handed hospitality helps make him an appealing character.

Penelope

In the opening chapters of *The Odyssey* Penelope is angry, frustrated, and helpless. She misses her husband, Odysseus. She worries about the safety of her son, Telemakhos. Her house is overrun with arrogant men who are making love to her servants and eating her out of house and home, all the while saying that they are courting her. She doesn't want to marry any of them, and their rude behavior can hardly be called proper courtship. She has wealth and position; she has beauty and intelligence; most of all she has loyalty to her husband. But against this corrupt horde who gather in her courtyard shooting dice, throwing the discus, killing her husband's cattle for their feasts, and drinking his wine, she is powerless.

After the beggar—Odysseus in disguise—arrives at Ithaka, we see more of Penelope's warmth, intelligence, and beauty. Within the limits of behavior available to her as a woman at that time, she is extraordinary. She is a match for Odysseus.

The Gods

The Odyssey is filled with gods. The "father of men and gods" is **Zeus,** whose might is expressed by his use of thunder and lightning. His less terrifying directives are delivered by the gods' messenger, **Hermes.** On Mount Olympos where the gods live, Zeus will have the last word. But in the meantime even he can't always control the actions of other powerful gods, such as **Poseidon,** the god of the sea, whose wrath Odysseus incurred.

Pallas Athena (usually just called Athena), "the grey-eyed goddess," is a dominant figure in *The Odyssey*. She personifies wisdom, and often seems to play the part of self-control in relation to Odysseus. **Apollo,** the god of manly youth, beauty, poetry, and music, is mentioned. Later in Classical Greece, Apollo became associated with the sun, but in Homeric times **Helios** is the sun god. It is his cattle that are slaughtered by Odysseus' men, causing his wrath. Helios gets Zeus to wreck Odysseus' ship in revenge.

OTHER CHARACTERS

The Family of Odysseus

In addition to Penelope and Telemakhos, the family of Odysseus includes his elderly father, **Laertes,** who appears at the end of the story for a reunion with his son.

Friends of Odysseus

Mentes and **Mentor** are old family friends who come to the aid of Telemakhos with advice in the absence of his father. **Halitherses** is another friend.

Servants of Odysseus

A loyal member of the household is **Eurykleia,** "the dear old nurse." She has been in the family for years and it is reported that Odysseus never slept with her, wanting not to anger his wife. It is an honor for a woman of the lower ranks to be invited to bed by a man of the nobility, just as it is an honor for a god to sleep with a mortal. Odysseus' sensitivity to his wife's feelings in the matter of Eurykleia is exceptional. It also keeps peace in the house.

Philoitios, the cattle foreman or cowherd, and **Eumaios,** the swineherd, are servants faithful to Odysseus. In contrast, **Melanthios,** the goatherd, insults Odysseus and steals weapons from the storehouse to help the suitors. His disloyalty is severely punished.

The Suitors

The men who lead "the wolfish troop" of more than a hundred suitors are **Antinoos** and **Eurymakhos. Amphinomos,** another suitor, reveals some

sense of conscience during the plot to murder Telemakhos, when he observes that "it is a shivery thing to
kill a prince of royal blood."

Crewmen to Telemakhos and Odysseus

Peiraios is Telemakhos' crewman, entrusted to
keep Telemakhos' gifts from Menelaos while Telemakhos asserts himself against the suitors. **Eurylokhos**
is Odysseus' right-hand man; he is also the one who
leads the men to kill and eat the sacred cattle of
Helios. Eurylokhos dies in the ensuing shipwreck.
Another of Odysseus' shipmates is **Elpenor,** who falls
off the roof, drunk, while at the home of Kirke. He
breaks his neck and dies. Odysseus sees his ghost in
the underworld.

Army Friends of Odysseus

Nestor, the first of Odysseus' army friends to be
visited by Telemakhos, is called "Nestor of Gerenia,"
"Neleus' son," and "prince of charioteers." He was
the chief adviser of the Greek forces. His son, **Peisistratos,** becomes Telemakhos' good friend.

The Shades in the Place of the Dead

In the course of Book 11 Odysseus visits Erebos, a
realm of darkness, the place of the dead. **Hades,** the
god of the underworld, is called "Death" in the Fitzgerald translation. **Persephone** is the occasional and
unwilling bride of Death.

In the place of the dead, Odysseus meets the ghost
of his mother, **Antikleia,** the daughter of **Autolykos.**
He also greets **Teiresias,** the blind soothsayer of
Thebes. He sees **Epicaste,** (Jocasta), mother of **Oidipous;** (Oedipus); **Leda,** to whom Zeus made love in
the form of a swan; **Ariadne,** daughter of King **Minos,**

who helped **Theseus** through the labyrinth; King Minos himself; as well as **Orion,** the famous hunter; **Tantolos,** who is punished by having water just out of reach of his thirsting mouth; and **Sisyphos,** whose punishment is eternally to push a boulder up hill only to have it roll back down. The muscle man of many legends, **Herakles,** is there too, as is **Agamemnon.**

Akhilleus (Achilles)

In the underworld Odysseus sees also the shade of Akhilleus, who went to Troy knowing he would be killed, but preferred honorable death on the battlefield to an ignominious life. At first he sulked in his tent, refusing to fight, because he had not been awarded the woman **Briseis** as part of his share of the spoils of war. Later he killed **Hector,** the Trojan champion, in single combat, moved to action out of anger and grief over the death of his friend, **Patroklos.** At Troy, Akhilleus died when shot in the heel, his only vulnerable spot, the place covered by his mother's hand when she dipped him for protection into the River Styx, which separates the land of the living from the land of the dead. **Paris,** who stole Helen, shot the arrow that killed Akhilleus.

The Phaiakians

The "people of the sea," the Phaiakians, live on Skheria island, governed by King **Alkinoos** and his wife **Arete.** Their daughter is the princess **Nausikaa.** Nausikaa is portrayed as young, virginal, bright, and lovely. Skheria is where Odysseus ends up after his final shipwreck and where he tells the story of his adventures.

The Characters Odysseus Meets During His Adventures

Finally there is the assortment of gods, demigods, monsters, witches, nymphs and others, encountered by Odysseus on his travels. These are, in chronological order, the **Kikones** at Ismaros; the **Lotos Eaters** and their dreamy ways; **Aiolos,** the king of the winds, on Aiolia Island; the murderous **Laistrygonians;** **Kirke,** who can change men into swine; the **Seirenes,** with their alluring voices; **Skylla** the cliff and **Kharybdis** the whirlpool; **Helios,** the god of the sun; and **Kalypso** on Ogygia.

Other Elements

SETTING

Present action takes place at Mount Olympos, the home of the gods; in Ithaka, Odysseus' island kingdom; at Pylos with Nestor, and Sparta with Menelaos; on Kalypso's island, Ogygia; and on Skheria island, where Alkinoos reigns. During the flashback on Skheria when Odysseus relates the story of his wanderings, a number of other settings are described as Odysseus moves from Troy, through the Mediterranean, to Ogygia.

THEMES

1. THE QUEST OF TELEMAKHOS

Scholars call Books 1–4 the *Telemacheia,* since it is the story of Telemakhos' education and maturation as he moves out into the world. The standard term for a novel depicting a young person's education is the German *Bildungsroman.*

2. THE WANDERINGS OF ODYSSEUS

In these folkloric adventures the hero is repeatedly tested and stretched by all that nature, man, and the supernatural world can throw against him.

3. HOMECOMING, VENGEANCE, AND THE RESTORATION OF ORDER

The trial of the bow and axes was originally folklore. The theme of the faithful wife occurs in many legends.

4. LOYALTY

Loyalty is most apparent in Penelope's resisting of the suitors, but it is a trait essential to all the characters in Odysseus' family. For twenty years Odysseus never stops wanting to return home. Telemakhos will not send his mother back to her father and force her to choose another husband. Instead, he sets out to find news of his father. The servants Eurykleia and Eumaios are also important exemplars of loyalty. Athena's devotion to Odysseus is another.

5. HOSPITALITY

This is the sign of a civilized society. Telemakhos shows hospitality to Athena and to his father in disguise. He receives it on his visits to Nestor and Menelaos. Alkinoos extends hospitality to Odysseus, as do Kalypso and (after some initial unpleasantness) Kirke. Contrasting examples of suspicion, hostility, and barbarity abound, showing up in their most extreme form as cannibalism.

6. INTELLIGENCE

The ability to solve problems is vital to an epic hero. Odysseus, as James Joyce put it, invented the first tank when he devised the Trojan horse. Penelope's ruse of unweaving the shroud shows her intelligence.

Odysseus' quick wit and invention of believable lies, helping him to conceal his identity and assess situations, are much admired by Athena.

7. EXPERIENCE
Both Telemakhos and Odysseus are men of action who learn about the world and themselves through travel to new lands, conversations with strangers, having adventures, and being tested.

8. RESPECT FOR THE GODS, ORDER, FATE
These linked concepts provide the underpinning for the entire book. Klytaimnestra, Agamemnon's wife, is no respecter of the right order of things, or of the gods. Her murder of her husband is an example of lack of order, and it causes a chain of further dreadful events. Her son, Orestes, must kill Klytaimnestra in revenge and is then hounded for the rest of his life by the avenging spirits called the Furies, for committing that horrible but necessary deed.

Odysseus' men defy the gods by eating Helios' forbidden cattle. It is only through the intervention of Athena that Odysseus is spared and allowed to return to his home, where the invasion of the suitors is portrayed as disorderly, chaotic, and wrong. Odysseus must struggle, suffer, and be obedient to the gods, but he cannot escape his fate any more than the suitors can escape theirs.

STYLE

Greek epic poetry was written in *dactylic hexameter:* ⁻ ′ ′. Each line had five dactylic feet and a sixth spondaic foot consisting of two strong beats: ⁻ ⁻. Longfellow's "Evangeline" is written in dactyls: "Thīs ís thĕ fōrést prímēvál." Because this beat gets sing-songy in English, Fitzgerald and other verse translators use the most common meter of English poetry, *iambic pentameter:* "Ī plēdged thēse rītes, thēn slāshed thē lāmb ānd ēwē," varying it to avoid monotony.

Epithets are descriptive tags attached to persons, places, or things: rosy-fingered Dawn, sandy Pylos, wine-dark sea. These helped the poet-composer fill out a line of verse without throwing off his meaning. *Epic similes* are long comparisons used to make the poet's meaning vivid. Odysseus returning home to rout the suitors is compared to a lion finding fawns in his den and attacking them. Some of these epic similes are set pieces that give the poet a breather. *Irony* heightens the drama of the story. The audience often knows Odysseus is actually present, but the characters do not. *Repetition* is part of oral tradition. The ears lose anything spoken only once, so the poet repeats.

POINT OF VIEW

Everything in the story is told by Homer, speaking as a mouthpiece for the Muse, faithfully retelling the legends of the past. So when a character talks, his or her words come through Homer and the conversation tends to be in long, rather formal speeches rather than quick dialogue. The poet-narrator's eyes see past and present as equally interesting and valuable. Sometimes a dramatic scene—such as the bathing of Odysseus' feet by Eurykleia when she sees his scar and discovers his true identity—will be interrupted by a long story from the past about how he got the scar.

The Story

BOOK 1: A GODDESS INTERVENES

The first thing the poet-narrator does is ask the Muse to help him tell his tale. In Greek mythology the Muses, the daughters of Memory, inspire the arts. Homer wants the Muse to speak through him so his story will be true to the legends of the past.

Next comes a brief summary of Odysseus' wanderings since he left Troy twenty years ago. He is now on Kalypso's island of Ogygia, where he has been for the last eight years.

NOTE: If this seems like a long time for an epic hero to be dilly-dallying, remember that the gods have to help you, and you have to deserve their help, or you're stuck. This is Poseidon's punishment which, after all, Odysseus deserved. Remember, too, that Kalypso is very attractive.

Now, however, Poseidon is away at a banquet, enjoying the offerings of roast meat dedicated to him. Perhaps while his back is turned Odysseus can reach home.

After the invocation and summary, Mount Olympos is the first real scene. Zeus tells the story of Agamemnon. (Homer will use this story again later because it is the opposite of Odysseus' story.) Klytaimnestra's faithlessness contrasts with Penelope's constancy. Agamemnon is murdered, whereas Odysseus kills the lawless suitors. Orestes' painful role as avenger of his father's death contrasts with Telemakhos' achievement of manhood at his father's side.

Athena speaks up for her favorite, Odysseus, and Zeus agrees to send a message to Kalypso to let Odysseus go.

NOTE: Although this is the story of Odysseus and Telemakhos, the first character to speak is Zeus. This gives you an idea of just how important gods and goddesses were to the Greeks.

A sailor's image shows Odysseus' yearning for home, his desire "to see the hearthsmoke leaping upward from his own island." It's something you would see from your ship far away on the ocean when the island is only a dot on the horizon.

Scene two takes place in Ithaka where we get our first look at Penelope's suitors. Notice what they're doing and whose cattle are being killed for their feast. We also get our first impression of Telemakhos, and it's an important one because as soon as Athena comes to him (she's disguised but he recognizes her), he begins to mature quickly. Here he is inactive, wistful, boyish.

NOTE: One of the Greek ideals is open-handed hospitality to strangers, no questions asked. Telemakhos lives up to the ideal. You may notice a tendency in the poem to idealize these Greek noblemen and their possessions. The dishes and furnishings mentioned here are perfect. Do you enjoy these descriptions, or would you rather see a few worn or tarnished household items?

The purpose of Book 1 is evident in the conversation between Telemakhos and Athena. When he sounds wistful, wanting a father, her response is, "You are a child no longer." His problems aren't going to solve themselves. He must act. He should call an assembly to try to get help in Ithaka. He should also set out with a ship and crew to learn about the world and find news of his father.

Telemakhos could tell Athena to mind her own business. He could refuse to take any adult actions. But Athena is really an embodiment of his own good sense. He rises to the challenge and even realizes that a god has spoken to him.

We now get our first glimpse of Penelope, who, when the bard, Phemios, sings of Troy, cannot bear to hear the song. The last time she saw Odysseus was twenty years ago when he left home to fight the Trojan War.

NOTE: Homer has set up an ironic situation, where we know something that Penelope doesn't—that Odysseus is alive. The audience likes to feel "in the know" compared to the characters. There's also a small joke in having Homer tell a story of Troy in which another poet (Phemios) tells a story of Troy.

Telemakhos smoothly conceals from Penelope's suitor Antinoos the fact that his visitor was an immortal. Telemakhos' father, Odysseus, is much admired by Athena for his ability to come up with a cool, false story. Like father, like son.

BOOK 2: A HERO'S SON AWAKENS

Book 2 takes place in Ithaka. Homer signals that a new day has begun by referring to the dawn. Like the sea, the seasons, and other forces of nature, she is one of the immortals, complete with "fingers of pink light." Without alarm clocks or electricity, people in 750 B.C. would have been attuned to dawn's chasing away the darkness each morning.

There's much detail about the family of old Aigyptos. People are almost always identified in terms of their families, and Homer doesn't mind interrupting his narrative to fill us in on a new character's background.

Antinoos tells about Penelope's trick. She said she would choose one of the suitors to marry when she finished weaving a shroud for her father-in-law. But every night she unraveled that day's weaving.

At the assembly, Antinoos blames Penelope for the suitors' bad behavior. If Telemakhos wants to restore order to his house, he should send his mother back to her father's house and make her choose a new husband. Telemakhos' loyalty to his mother shows in his refusal.

When Telemakhos begs Zeus for a slaughter of the suitors, Zeus sends an omen instead: two eagles drop on the suitors, "wielding their talons, tearing cheeks and throats." The eagle, a bird of prey, is considered kingly. This is the first of many omens that Odysseus will return and have justice. The suitors don't notice the omen, being so arrogant that they're blind to all warnings.

When this book ends, Telemakhos has obeyed Athena's two orders—to hold an assembly, and to set sail into the world.

NOTE: Notice how he handles the mockery of Antinoos back at his home after the assembly. Antinoos would love to make Telemakhos lose his self-control. Keep in mind that Telemakhos is about twenty years old and the suitors are much older. What do you think would happen here if Telemakhos threw a punch, instead of calmly withdrawing his hand from Antinoos' hand?

Telemakhos and his crew, accompanied by Athena (still disguised), sail all night and arrive the next morning at the home of Nestor in Pylos.

BOOK 3: LORD OF THE WESTERN APPROACHES

Book 3 begins at dawn. Nestor's people are gathered on the shore to sacrifice respectfully to the gods and then to feast.

As Telemakhos approaches Nestor, you can tell from what Athena says to him that he must be feeling awkward in front of this wise, old, famous king, a friend of his father but someone he hasn't ever met. He's afraid he won't say the right thing. This is another test of his ability to handle things as an adult.

Observe Peisistratos, Nestor's youngest son, graciously makes the guests welcome. His request that the disguised Athena offer the prayer sets up a humorously ironic situation. Athena is offering a prayer to herself, which she then grants.

NOTE: These well-mannered people make the guests comfortable and give them wine and food. Talk and questions come later. Their ways are different from ours. We usually want to know who somebody is and what he does for a living before we're willing to invite him to dinner. Notice how Telemakhos handles himself when he's finally asked why he's come.

Homer whets your appetite for Odysseus' appearance by having other characters talk about him. Nestor says, "He had no rivals, your father, at the tricks of war." Nestor also compliments Telemakhos on being "tall and well set-up," well built. This statement about his manly appearance must make him feel good, especially after so many insults from the suitors.

Nestor has no direct news of Odysseus, but he tells what happened to other Greeks after the war. He relates the story of Agamemnon's murder, which you heard at the start of Book 1. He says Menelaos was detained in Egypt on the way home, but managed to make a fortune while stuck there. Nestor suggests that Telemakhos visit Menelaos for further news, and offers a chariot, horses, and the company of his son, Peisistratos. Athena says Telemakhos should accept and that she will stay with the ship. Athena leaves the company quickly, in the form of a seahawk, and all now realize that Athena has been among them. A young cow with gold foil on her horns will be sacrificed the next day in Athena's honor.

Another dawn. The sacrifice is carried out, involving flowers, water, and a basket of barley. Nestor's son Thrasymedes does the slaughtering himself, not a priest or servant, and the butchering details are vivid. You might ask yourself why the women wail with joy.

At the close of the book, after another feast, Telemakhos and Peisistratos drive off in high style in the chariot lent them by Nestor. Compare Telemakhos' experiences with Nestor to those in Ithaka among the suitors. He has been accepted and admired. He has spoken and acted well. He drives off in the equivalent of Nestor's Cadillac with a friend of his own age and class. Homer never says, "Telemakhos was happy," but he doesn't need to. You can feel that relief and happiness when the thoroughbreds with their streaming manes prance off.

NOTE: A storyteller has to be aware of pace, of building the action to a climax and not letting the tension flag. Telemakhos' visit at Pylos was full of satisfactions, but compared to the visit with Menelaos, it was fairly low key. Menelaos is younger, richer, and more expressive than Nestor. It was his wife Helen's abduction that caused the Trojan War. It was his brother who was murdered when he returned from that war. Menelaos' friends suffered and died on his account. He grieves for them. He doesn't say it, but perhaps he grieves so much because he feels responsible.

BOOK 4: THE RED-HAIRED KING AND HIS LADY

The emotional pitch of Book 4 is higher than that of Book 3. You see many tears and extravagant gifts, you hear many stories and an invitation to stay not just overnight but for eleven or twelve days. Then, at the height of Telemakhos' acceptance by Menelaos as the son of his dear friend, and as a worthy person in his own right, Homer dramatically shifts the scene back to Ithaka and shows us the suitors plotting Telemakhos' murder.

The visit to Menelaos even begins at a high level of emotion—Telemakhos walks into a double wedding for Menelaos' son and daughter, complete with a banquet, minstrel, and tumblers. The theme of hospitality is sounded again when one of the king's companions-at-arms asks if the strangers should be invited in, considering the occasion, and is scolded for even asking. Of course they should. Nestor's home was extremely comfortable, but Menelaos' palace is grand. There's a nice bit of characterization showing Telemakhos' boyish reaction to all the elegance: he whispers to Peisistratos that he can hardly believe his eyes, all that bronze, gold, amber, silver, and ivory. Clearly Telemakhos and Peisistratos have become good friends.

Before knowing who his guests are, Menelaos begins to speak of Troy. It took him seven years to get home. He made a lot of money during his travels, but in the meantime his brother, Agamemnon, was murdered. He admits that he often weeps over the companions lost at Troy. He speaks of Odysseus and how much he misses his good friend. The irony of the situation is that he is speaking to Odysseus' son, which we know but he doesn't. On hearing about his father, Telemakhos weeps. The full range of emotions is open to both sexes in this world, and the losses of this war are as real as losses of friends in World War II, Korea, or Vietnam.

It is Helen who notices Telemakhos' tears and says he looks like Odysseus. Peisistratos says it is Telemakhos, and the extent of their friendship is shown when he adds "but he is gentle, and would be ashamed to clamor for attention before your grace." Menelaos, of course, is overjoyed. He was so close to Odysseus that he had hoped to convince him to move near to him. "I could have cleaned out one of my towns to be his new domain," he says. This remark shows not only his extravagant nature, but gives you an idea of the power kings of this rank wielded. But Menelaos' love for Odysseus is deep, and his words and his pain at the loss of his friend bring grief to everyone. Husband, wife, and guests all cry, for Peisistratos, too, lost a brother at Troy.

Peisistratos calls the group out of its sorrow, for the hour is late. Menelaos compliments him on his wisdom. Supper is eaten, and Helen drugs the wine with a potion to induce forgetfulness and drive away sadness. Over supper she tells Telemakhos how Odysseus sneaked into Troy during the siege, disguised as a beggar, but that she recognized him. Another story, in which you learn about our hero before you meet him, is told by Menelaos. While the Greeks hid inside the Trojan horse, Helen walked around it, patting it and calling out, making her voice sound like the voices of the wives the Greeks had left behind. One of the Greek soldiers was about to call out when Odysseus clapped his hand over the man's mouth. This story makes us realize that Menelaos and Odysseus are really fox-hole buddies, men who've been through life-and-death situations together and who have a special kind of love. The party breaks up on a happier note and everyone retires for the night.

Dawn again. It gets to be a cliché after a while, but the "finger tips of rose" serve as a time marker for the listener who has to keep track of everything by memory. Now King Menelaos comes to Telemakhos, and in an honest display of affection asks him why he's come. "I came to hear what news you had of Father," Telemakhos says simply. He explains the situation at home. Menelaos' angry reaction must be satisfying to Telemakhos.

NOTE: Menelaos' reaction also contains the first epic simile you have heard so far, eight lines comparing the suitors to soft, weak fawns in a lion's den. The lion will return to bring them doom.

Menelaos' news comes from a reliable source, Proteus, the "Ancient of the Sea" who has the gift of prophecy. Proteus told him that Aias bragged he had beaten the gods and the sea—and was drowned. Agamemnon was murdered (Menelaos cried at the news). And Odysseus was held on Kalypso's island. Menelaos continues his story with an invitation to Telemakhos to stay, and an offer of almost embarrassingly rich gifts: a chariot, three horses, and a hammered cup. Telemakhos refuses gracefully.

NOTE: You may think it strange that Homer doesn't interrupt Menelaos to give us Telemakhos' reaction to this news that his father is alive. This is the first solid information he's gotten; you would think we'd see Telemakhos' response. Scholars have said that sometimes "Homer nods," that is, nods off to sleep. Perhaps this is one of the places where the poet dozes.

Telemakhos accepts a silver wine bowl and the long scene ends with preparations for yet another feast.

Meanwhile, back in Ithaka the suitors amuse themselves throwing a discus and javelins. They learn from the man who lent Telemakhos his ship that Telemakhos has gone. They feel Telemakhos has defied them and plan an ambush at sea on his return. Medon, the crier, tells Penelope of their plan, an act that may save his life later on. Penelope is upset and angry, frustrated and helpless. We know Athena will save Telemakhos, but Penelope needs to know that as well. So Athena sends her a comforting dream. The book ends with a cliff-hanger, as Antinoos launches his ship for the ambush. Thus ends the opening section, which focuses on the secondary hero, Telemakhos.

BOOK 5: SWEET NYMPH AND OPEN SEA

Scene one of Book 5 is set back on Mount Olympos. You get a brief recap of Athena telling Zeus that Odysseus needs to be allowed to go home. Athena adds that now, to complicate matters, the suitors are lying in ambush for Telemakhos. Zeus foretells Odysseus' future and sends Hermes to Kalypso's island. Watch to see if what Zeus says comes true, or if Odysseus manages to do some things his own way.

NOTE: A storyteller draws you into the situations he describes by appealing to your senses: touch, smell, taste, sight, hearing. The description of Kalypso's cave in scene two is full of sensory details. It's also a strange mix of the exotic and familiar. Notice that hospitality is offered even by a nymph to the messenger of the gods—nectar and ambrosia, the gods' special drink and food.

At last you meet Odysseus, when Kalypso comes to tell him to build a raft because he is free to go. Later Odysseus and Kalypso share a meal. In an amusing scene, he eats people food and she eats goddess food. "Then each one's hands went out on each one's feast." Perhaps his mortality and her immortality is the reason why these two cannot stay together.

NOTE: Kalypso offers Odysseus immortality if he will stay. Would you turn down eternal youth and life? What can you tell about Odysseus because of his rejection of her offer?

Kalypso is certainly appealing. She is "divinely made," which means she has the figure of a goddess. She has pretty braids, a warm, sweet voice, seductive ways. Odysseus continues to make love to her each night even though, you are told, he has grown tired of her and yearns for home. She teases Hermes when she says Odysseus is free to go but she, who has no ships, cannot "send" him. Obviously she wants him to stay. Notice especially her speech to Odysseus when she asks how he can prefer Penelope to her. This is their parting after eight years. Does she sound hurt and angry? Is he cruel? In modern terms, this is a moment of divorce, but a somewhat bittersweet parting, with little or no anger on either side.

The personal part of this book is followed by an adventurous part. Notice what Odysseus builds and how long it takes him. Again, you are not in the realm of realism but in the world of an idealized epic hero. Kalypso helps him, bearing no grudge. Then for seventeen days Odysseus sails freely until Poseidon arrives on the scene. Observe Odysseus' reaction to Ino's advice to let go of what's left of his ship and swim for it, using her veil for protection. He rarely accepts what he's told without weighing it carefully first. Is that "wisdom"?

He swims for two days. An epic simile describes how he feels when he finally sees land: the sight is as dear to him as a sick father's return to health is to his children. Yet he is at something of a loss when he encounters the steep cliffs and rocky shore.

NOTE: Homer was no landlubber: he knew surf, rocks, currents, undertow, tides. Athena helps Odysseus find the river's mouth, but Odysseus is the one who thinks to pray to the river. Nature in this world is respected as man's equal or superior.

Odysseus swims to shore during the still water, a short period between the ebb and flow of the tide. He returns Ino's veil. Homer does a good job of making you feel how worn out and water-logged he is. He could easily die, even now that he's reached the "safety" of land, of exhaustion and exposure, but his "tough heart" can endure still more and his clever brain finds a protected place for him to sleep. It is a relief for the reader, too, when he finally crawls into his bed of leaves and falls asleep.

BOOK 6: THE PRINCESS AT THE RIVER

Book 6 is many people's favorite. The Princess Nausikaa is delightful, and her meeting with the grizzled, naked "war veteran" is funny and charming.

Homer begins with a brief history of the Phaiakians, then shifts to a scene of Nausikaa asleep in her bed, a tender way of starting off. Athena, in yet another disguise, comes to Nausikaa in a dream, in the form of one of her girl friends. That's how Nausikaa gets the idea of washing the marriage linen. When she asks her father to give her a cart and mules for this project, she sounds sweetly self-important, bustling, housewifely. Notice her blush. She has marriage on her mind—preparing the linen is not just a service she's doing for her brothers or the family in general. She is obviously a much loved and indulged daughter. She is equipped with mules and cart, her maids to help her, and a picnic lunch. They even take olive oil for rubbing onto their skins after bathing. This trip to wash the linen is more than just doing the laundry.

The freshness of detail is what makes the outing so appealing. The sheets are washed and spread on the beach to dry. The girls swim, rub themselves with oil, eat the food, and play ball. Does this feel like 750 B.C.? Yes, they washed the clothes in the river, but the tone makes it seem very recent. All the girls need is a Frisbee instead of a ball. Girls playing catch today might shriek if one of them threw the ball into the river by mistake. Having Odysseus awaken to that shout is much more interesting and dramatic than if he woke just because the sun came up or because he was hungry.

NOTE: Try to visualize the meeting that results. Put yourself in Nausikaa's shoes, or put yourself in Odysseus' (of course he isn't wearing any, or anything else for that matter, which is part of what makes the encounter so entertaining). Up until now you've heard of Odysseus in war situations, watched him with a lover, Kalypso, seen him as a man of action battling the sea. What do you think of his behavior toward Nausikaa, the decisions he makes as to how to approach her, the words he chooses? If you and your friends were playing ball in a remote area and a bearded, rough-looking, naked man suddenly came out of the bushes, how would you respond?

Observe Nausikaa's behavior and her words to Odysseus. The hospitality theme occurs again: "Strangers and beggars come from Zeus." Observe, too, Odysseus' delicacy of feeling in declining to bathe naked before these young girls. He knows how to behave with women (remember his tact with Kalypso). He impresses Nausikaa so much that she says, "I wish my husband could be as fine as he." Homer hints deliciously at the possibility of a match between these two, which makes the story more fun. You *know* he will return to his wife, but you can still *imagine* that he will fall in love with Nausikaa. It's not an appropriate match, though. Nausikaa is young enough to be Odysseus' daughter, and he has lived too long and been through too much to find lasting appeal in youthful innocence. An affair with Nausikaa is out of the question. But Homer lets us flirt with the idea by showing that romance is on Nausikaa's mind. That may be why she tells Odysseus to come to her father's palace alone to avoid gossip. There's nothing to gossip about, except perhaps in her own mind!

The book ends with Odysseus praying to Athena for love and mercy from these people. His praying is an example of proper behavior. Epic hero though he is, he must not swagger into the court of Alkinoos expecting to be treated royally. He is a stranger and alone. One of his attractive qualities is his vulnerability despite his enormous strength. He also knows that no matter how wealthy or powerful a man is, he is still mortal and must never forget that fate is in the hands of the gods. Athena hears his prayer.

BOOK 7: GARDENS AND FIRELIGHT

In Book 7 Nausikaa returns home. Her brothers greet her and stable the mules and help unload the laundry. Nausikaa's withdrawal to her room suggests that she has been affected by her meeting with Odysseus.

When Odysseus enters the town, Athena meets him in yet another disguise, this time as a small girl in pigtails hugging a water jug. How does this role make you feel about this grey-eyed goddess of wisdom who usually carries a long spear and often is involved in warfare? In this disguise Athena gives Odysseus some background about the people he is about to meet. She says Arete, the queen, is a person of compassion—Odysseus should address himself to her.

In describing the palace of Alkinoos and Arete, Homer outdoes himself: bronze-paneled walls, azure molding made of lapis lazuli, sculpture, gold and silver everywhere, even in the door handles. The torchbearers, the maids grinding corn and weaving, the well-tended orchard filled with fragrant fruit—the place is a model of industry and comfort. When Odysseus approaches Arete, he kneels in front of her and puts his arms around her knees in a gesture that asks for mercy. Remember that he chose not to approach Nausikaa this way. Then the gesture would have been awkward and might have been misinterpreted. But here the gesture of humility is the right thing to do.

The rituals of hospitality to a stranger are observed, including a libation, the spilling out of some wine as a sacrifice to the gods before drinking the remainder. A realistic moment occurs when Odysseus apologizes for continuing to eat, while reassuring Alkinoos that he is not a god in disguise. He is starving and, he says, "Belly must be filled." He also asks for passage home the next day.

When all have gone to bed except the king and queen, Odysseus describes how he came to Skheria and explains that Nausikaa helped him—a fact that accounts for the fine clothes he is wearing. Nausikaa's father finds fault with her behavior. She should have brought Odysseus directly home with her. Notice how smoothly Odysseus covers the situation, taking responsibility for his arriving alone. He makes no mention of "gossip." He will give Nausikaa no reason to be embarrassed.

NOTE: What do you make of Alkinoos' response, which is, in short order, to offer Odysseus Nausikaa as his wife? Do you think this father, who observed his daughter's blush only this morning, is sensitive to the fact that she might have a crush on this hand- some, though middle-aged and weathered stranger? Alkinoos also offers Odysseus swift passage home, if that should be his choice. This is a delicate conversa- tion between two men of the world. Odysseus doesn't actually refuse the offer of Nausikaa, but he heartily accepts the offer of passage home, calling down Zeus' blessing on Alkinoos. Diplomatic is too mild a word for Odysseus. He makes everyone feel good, offends nobody, and gets what he wants.

Many beds are described in *The Odyssey*, but the one prepared for Odysseus at the end of this book is especially soft and inviting. Perhaps this is because he has not slept in a bed for twenty days, not since he left Kalypso.

BOOK 8: THE SONGS OF THE HARPER

At dawn in Book 8, Athena, disguised this time as a crier, draws a crowd of citizens, announcing the pres- ence of a stranger in town. Alkinoos asks for volun- teers to crew the visitor home, and invites the citizens to a feast at the palace. Animals are sacrificed and cooked for the banquet. A blind poet (an earlier tradi- tion said that Homer was blind, though modern scholarship does not support this idea) sings a song of Troy, making Odysseus cry. You can see how Homer is building up to the revelation of the stranger's identity.

NOTE: The Phaiakians participate in games like a modern track meet. The nautical names of the participants make us aware that they know the sea—the "winedark," "violet," "foaming" sea, as Homer calls it. We have names that mean occupations, too, such as "Smith" and "Wheelwright," but they don't have much impact when Mr. Smith sells real estate and Ms. Wheelwright manages a bank.

When the stranger is invited by Seareach to participate in the games, he refuses, saying he is too preoccupied with his troubles and too eager to go home. Seareach doesn't like this answer. He insults Odysseus, saying he refused because he is a bum with no athletic skill. Naturally Odysseus is provoked and proceeds to hurl a discus farther than anyone else. Angry, he challenges all comers in racing, wrestling, boxing, archery, anything but sprinting—he says his legs have been made flabby by so many years at sea.

Alkinoos' answer is tactful. The Phaiakians are not boxers, he says. They like to race on land or sea. They especially like feasting, storytelling, dance, and song. The bard is called again and tells the story of Aphrodite's infidelity with Ares. It's a risqué story, perhaps chosen to divert the ruffled guest. Aphrodite's husband, the crippled god of the forge, Hephaistos, fashions a net that snares the guilty pair while they are making love. They cannot move apart or get up. Then Hephaistos invites the other gods to come and look.

NOTE: This story is told in *The Iliad* as well. It may be one of the set pieces Homer inserts into his narrative, giving himself a breather while entertaining his audience with what was apparently a popular tale.

Dancers and jugglers entertain the guests. Then Alkinoos calls for twelve lords, and himself to make thirteen, each to give Odysseus a cloak, a tunic, and a bar of gold. Alkinoos calls on Seareach to apologize, which he does with good grace, giving Odysseus a broadsword. Alkinoos gives Odysseus his own gold wine cup. From Odysseus' tears, Alkinoos may already have guessed who he is. These are extremely generous gifts.

A bath is provided for Odysseus, and his gifts are stowed for later travel. When he emerges from the bath and is dressed in a fresh tunic and cloak, he sees Nausikaa shyly waiting beside a pillar to say goodbye. Notice what each one says. Women of all ages and sorts seem to find Odysseus irresistible, and he adroitly manages not to break their hearts.

At the dinner banquet Odysseus cuts a tasty morsel of pork from his own portion and has it sent to the bard as a little gift. Then he requests the story of the Trojan horse. The story makes him cry, and at last Alkinoos asks him straight out to tell who he is.

BOOK 9: NEW COASTS AND POSEIDON'S SON

In the opening lines of Book 9 Odysseus at last reveals his identity. He explains that he was detained by Kalypso and by Kirke, but his loyalty to his home and Penelope was never in question because "in my heart I never gave consent." Do you accept that statement?

The closeness of life to nature in this world is shown in the encounter with the Kikones. Odysseus, the captain, cannot control his hungry men. In the world as Odysseus knows it, food comes from farming. Sunset is "unyoking time." If you're hungry, you don't go out for a fast-food hamburger. You catch, kill, butcher, cook, and eat a cow.

The greed of the men results in the loss of seventy-two of the company. "Six benches were left empty in every ship," and they started out with twelve ships. These ships have both sails and oars.

After two days of storm followed by one day of sailing followed by nine days of strong currents and high winds, the ships arrive at the land of the Lotos-Eaters. Those who eat Lotos forget their homeland and long to stay forever. Does Lotos appeal to you? These men have been through a lot—maybe Lotos stands for giving up the struggle.

NOTE: An epic hero is basically admirable, but he would be boring if he were perfect. The episode with the Kyklopes shows Odysseus at his best and worst. Sometimes a good characteristic, like curiosity, can also be a bad trait and cause a lot of trouble. The Kyklopes is not totally evil. Watch how he tends his sheep. Going about his duties in his dairy, he seems a good shepherd.

BOOK 10: THE GRACE OF THE WITCH

In Book 10 Aiolos gives Odysseus a bag containing the storm winds. Now he should be able to sail home safely. His company gets close enough to Ithaka to see men building fires on the shore. But Odysseus, not trusting anyone else, has steered alone for nine days.

He is exhausted, and he falls asleep. His men guess the bag holds gold or riches, and they open it. Whoosh—the ships are blown back to Aiolia. Aiolos now wants nothing to do with them. This incident seems to have a fairly neat moral.

Odysseus and his men run into more cannibalism, this time at the hands of the Laistrygonians. After two days beached and in despair, Odysseus climbs a hill, sees smoke, kills a deer, and comes back to his men with food. The men are fearful and wary after their experiences with the Kyklopes and the Laistrygonians, but they decide to investigate the smoke. Two platoons are formed, one led by Odysseus and the other by his lieutenant, Eurylokhos. Lots are shaken in a soldier's dogskin cap. Eurylokhos and his men are the ones to go out on patrol. They leave weeping with fear.

Like many of the female characters, Kirke is seen singing and weaving. She seems ordinary enough, except that at her feet lie tame wolves and mountain lions. When the men eat and drink what Kirke offers—all but Eurylokhos, who fears a trap—they are turned into swine. While nowadays you would take this metaphorically, Homer's audience took it literally.

Eurylokhos comes running back, scared to death. He gives a detailed report, including a description of Kirke's marble palace located in an open glade. He won't go back, he says, and he fears for Odysseus. But Odysseus must investigate.

Once again it's clear that it helps to have a god on your side. Hermes meets Odysseus and gives him a magic herb, moly, to protect him from Kirke's magic. He says to take out his sword if Kirke turns mean. Odysseus drinks Kirke's drink but it doesn't affect him. When she shakes her stick and orders him into the sty, he draws his sword. Suddenly she turns docile and clasps his knees. She recognizes him as Odysseus (his arrival was foretold to her by Hermes) and she invites him to bed! This is all rather sudden.

Odysseus won't consent unless she swears no foul play. She promises, and so they go to bed together. Afterward she bathes him luxuriously, gives him a tunic and cloak, and brings him food. He can't eat, out of grief for his men who are now in the form of pigs, so she restores them to human form and they are tearfully reunited with Odysseus. Kirke invites the entire company to stay.

Odysseus returns with this message to the rest of the men. The epic simile here describes the men as calves, bawling and bumping together, swarming around their mothers. It's interesting to think of Odysseus as "motherly." All return with him, though Eurylokhos resists, warns the others that Odysseus cannot always be trusted, and lags in the rear.

They stay a year, then yearn for home. As they get ready to leave, poor Elpenor falls off the roof and dies of a broken neck. He went up there, drunk, to sleep in the cool air and forgot where he was when he woke up. Kirke tells Odysseus he must next visit the land of the dead and speak with the blind prophet Teiresias. She gives detailed instructions about how he is to do this and even provides the sacrificial animals, a black ram and an ewe.

BOOK 11: A GATHERING OF SHADES

Odysseus follows all of Kirke's instructions. He sails to the proper place, digs a pit, sacrifices the ewe and ram, pours libations of milk, honey, and wine, sprinkles barley. He promises further sacrifices at Ithaka. The dead come and are kept at bay at sword's point. You were told all of this by Kirke in the previous book, but repetition in an oral story helps you keep track of things.

Elpenor appears first and pleads for a proper burning of his corpse and gear, and the building of a burial mound marked with his oar. The inclusion of Elpenor may remind you that not all soldiers die in glorious battle. Some succumb to the flu or fall off a roof because they are drunk. Odysseus weeps when he sees his mother, Antikleia. Then Teiresias comes.

Teiresias predicts more trouble from Poseidon. If the cattle of the sun god are eaten, all will perish but Odysseus. Teiresias describes the bad situation at home. He gives Odysseus his last assignment: from Ithaka he must travel inland with an oar over his shoulder until people take it for a winnowing fan. There, where people know nothing of the sea, he must make one final sacrifice to Poseidon. He will have a gentle seaborne death after a rich old age, leaving peace among his people. Through Teiresias, we get a glimpse of Odysseus as a tranquil old man.

This picture is quickly followed by one of a youthful Odysseus. After drinking the blood in the pit, Antikleia can speak and addresses Odysseus as "Child." He's probably about forty-five, but his mother's eyes remind you that he was once a boy. You have seen him as father, husband, son, military strategist, spy, lover, carpenter, beggar, athlete, sailor, captain, storyteller, mother to his men, liar—and here as a little boy.

NOTE: The meeting between mother and son is sad, for in his absence she died of loneliness for him, and though he cries and wishes to hold her and cry with her, he cannot because she no longer has a body.

The Akhaians are sensuous people who delight in love, fine clothes, baths, oil rubdowns, good stories, fleecy beds, delicious meats, breads, and wines. Death means to be deprived of all these pleasures— and of the simple comfort of touching a person you love.

Here in Hades Homer doesn't pass up the chance to insert many legends into his narrative. After Antikleia comes a long procession of famous women of the past and their stories.

Watch for a break in Odysseus' story. He falls silent and you are reminded that he is telling all of this to Arete and Alkinoos. Arete is impressed by him. She and Alkinoos say he must stay another day and offer even more gifts. Odysseus is gracious about prolonging his stay, and happy to go home with riches instead of empty handed. Alkinoos admires the honesty of Odysseus' story and the art with which he tells it. He wants to hear more, and asks about Odysseus' friends from Troy. That question is the transition back into the world of the dead.

Now comes the parade of famous men, led by the person whose story is most pertinent to that of Odysseus, Agamemnon. You've heard it twice before, but this time Agamemnon himself gets to tell it. His version is more complete and powerful, coming from the murdered man himself. A painful detail is that his wife murdered him before he got to see his only son. He asks Odysseus for news of Orestes. But alas, Odysseus knows nothing.

The dead may have no bodies, but it seems they keep their interest in the living. When Odysseus tells Akhilleus of his son's bravery and his getting through the war unscathed, Akhilleus is pleased. The dead continue to nurse grudges, as well. Aias is still angry at Odysseus because Odysseus got the weapons that had belonged to Akhilleus. Aias won't speak. It's a funny, human touch.

The Greek heroes are followed by other famous inhabitants of the underworld: Orion, Tantolos, Sisyphos, and Herakles. Odysseus waits in the hope of seeing one or two more, but he is suddenly surrounded by thousands of shades "rustling in a pandemonium of whispers." This moment is worthy of a first-rate horror movie—whispers are much more eerie than shouts. Odysseus can't wait to get out of there.

BOOK 12: SEA PERILS AND DEFEAT

Odysseus and his men return to Aiaia and take care of Elpenor's body as requested. While they rest, eat, and drink for a day, Kirke describes to Odysseus everything that will happen next and tells him what to do. Skylla is described as a yapping dog with twelve legs and six heads each with three rows of teeth. What do you think of Odysseus when he says he wants to fight Skylla? Notice Kirke's reaction and her advice: to fight Skylla is foolish; just row fast. Later, watch to see if he follows her advice or does what he wants to do.

By now you've heard so much about not eating the cattle of the sun god that you know for sure they will be eaten. The men have been warned. Odysseus has been warned. Why do mortals do the very things they have been told not to do?

Odysseus' curiosity shows itself again when he alone gets to hear the song of the Seirenes. He is not invulnerable to their enticing song, and cries out to be let loose from his protective bonds. The men keep rowing, with wax in their ears, and Eurylokhos and another man tie Odysseus with more rope to the mast. This time, although he exposes himself to danger because of his curiosity, he does not endanger his men as he did with the Kyklopes. When he confronts Skylla, he says he "forgets" Kirke's advice. Do you believe him?

NOTE: Since the temptation to eat the cattle of the sun god is so great a risk for these men, it would seem smart to stay away from them altogether. In many stories of ancient Greece there is a strong theme of fate as being something you cannot avoid. Remember in the famous Greek tragedy that Oedipus tries everything he can think of to avoid his fate of killing his father and marrying his mother, but it happens anyway. So, too, it seems as though Odysseus and his men cannot *not* go to the home of Helios. Everyone promises to stay clear of the cattle. But then they have a month of onshore gales, they eat all of their barley, and they are reduced to eating fish and sea birds: they're hungry. "Belly must be fed," Odysseus said earlier.

Of course Odysseus should not pick this moment to go inland to pray. Why couldn't he pray on shore? Of course he shouldn't fall asleep. Didn't you see this happen when the bag of winds was opened? Of course Eurylokhos should prevent the men from slaughtering the cattle, not lead them into it—but you have seen him oppose Odysseus' leadership before. The cattle are killed in a properly sacrificial manner, but that doesn't help. Odysseus knows he's in trouble the minute he smells roasting meat. Helios wants revenge. Zeus promises to strike the ship (they're down to one now, from twelve) with lightning.

An especially ghastly omen predicts what's coming. The hides crawl. The meat, raw and roasted, "moos" on the spits. When the men do set out, the ship is of course hit by lightning and all but Odysseus perish. He lashes the mast and keel together. He escapes Kharybdis, the whirlpool, by grabbing onto the fig tree over it. He washes up at Kalypso's island, Ogygia. Fate has played itself out. No one can escape what life has in store. The flashback is over.

BOOK 13: ONE MORE STRANGE ISLAND

When Odysseus, the master storyteller, finishes the flashback, the court of Alkinoos is spellbound—"no one stirred or sighed." Think what a compliment it is to the performers at the end of a play or concert if there's a moment of utter silence before the applause. Alkinoos calls on his lords for more gifts, a tripod and cauldron from each one.

NOTE: Alkinoos' remark that the people will be taxed to make up the loss reminds you that you're reading about a feudal society. The democracy of Classical Greece is far in the future, and even that democracy applied only to established male citizens. Slaves and women had no rights.

At dawn Odysseus' many gifts are brought to the ship and stowed. Thighbones are burned to the gods, everyone feasts, the bard sings again.

NOTE: You might do some research on the expression "winedark," which has puzzled scholars for hundreds of years. Homer usually uses it to describe the sea, but here in the epic simile (Odysseus hungers to leave for home as a farmer plowing all day hungers for his evening meal) it describes oxen.

Odysseus thanks and blesses Alkinoos and his people in a heartfelt speech. He gives special thanks to Arete. All are given wine so all may make libations before Odysseus' trip. There is something magical about the way Odysseus is rowed home asleep, and placed, still asleep with his treasure by him, in Phorkys cove at the foot of the olive tree near the cave of the immortal water nymphs, the Naiades. It almost suggests that he is about to waken from a long, incredible dream.

NOTE: The olive tree is a symbol of Athena and an essential element in Greek agricultural economy. Remember that Odysseus slept at the foot of one on Skheria, too.

Poseidon, in a brief scene with Zeus, makes it clear that he is not pleased that Odysseus' last voyage home was so easy. He wants to destroy the Phaiakians' ship and throw up a "mass of mountain in a ring around the city" so the Phaiakians will never sail again. Zeus suggests a milder punishment, to which Poseidon agrees: he lets the ship get within sight of the harbor and then turns it to stone.

Athena covers Ithaka with mist so that when Odysseus wakes he doesn't know where he is. He thinks the Phaiakians may have left him somewhere else, or even have stolen some of his treasure. Athena comes to him as a young shepherd. You have heard about

Ithaka before, but she gives the most detailed description yet. The island is too hilly and broken for horses and has no wide meadows, but it does have good soil, grain, wine, rainfall, pasture for oxen and goats, timber, and cattle ponds. The setting of the last half of the story is sharply drawn here.

Notice the false story Odysseus tells the "shepherd." He says the night of the supposed murder was murky, a detail to make the whole thing convincing. Athena is so pleased with his quick invention that she reveals herself to him as a tall, beautiful woman, "I that am always with you in times of trial." Still he doubts, and she likes his caution. She says he is the best of all men alive at plots and stories. His cool, quick detachment is the reason she can never forsake him.

She removes the mist, reveals the details of the cove and Mount Neion, "with his forest on his back." Apparently the islands of the Mediterranean were heavily wooded once, though today many of them are barren. She helps him hide his gifts in the cave and reminds him that for the past three years the suitors have plagued his wife and eaten up his stores and cattle. He realizes he would have wound up like Agamemnon if she hadn't helped him, and begs her to fight at his side in the approaching battle.

Her plan is to disguise him. He must join the swineherd first. Meanwhile she will go to Sparta and fetch Telemakhos home. She turns Odysseus into a bald, wrinkled, bleary-eyed beggar. She dresses him in a filthy tunic, tattered, greasy, and stained. She gives him a mangy buckskin cloak, a staff, and a "leaky knapsack with no strap but a loop of string." Who would guess this wretched beggar is the king? Be prepared for one ironic situation after another.

BOOK 14: HOSPITALITY IN THE FOREST

Taking a stony trail into the hills, Odysseus comes to the stone hut of Eumaios. It's timbered with wild pear wood, fenced by an oak palisade, and overlooks twelve sties containing fifty sows with piglets, and 360 boars. Four dogs guard the pigs and four boys help Eumaios as underherdsmen. Three of the boys are pasturing herds in the woods when Odysseus approaches, and the other one has been sent to town with a fat boar for the suitors. What do you think of Odysseus' sitting down and dropping his stick when attacked by the dogs? Would you have done that?

NOTE: Homer has a special tenderness for Eumaios and breaks out of the narrative voice to address him directly—"O my swineherd!"—as though the swineherd were sitting next to him or as though the memory of the swineherd overcomes him with emotion. Some people find this distracting and sentimental. Others find it touching.

The swineherd is an exaggerated example of the faithful servant. He mentions the absence of his true master in his first speech to the stranger even though his master's been away twenty years. He uses tips of fir under his own bedcovering to make Odysseus a couch. He expresses anger at the suitors and is sour about the rewards he would have gotten if his master had stayed at home. He kills and cooks two young pigs to give Odysseus food, mentioning that wandering men often get new clothes from Penelope in exchange for "news" of her missing husband.

We get a picture of Odysseus as an easy and much-loved master, for the swineherd misses him more than he misses his own parents. The irony of the scene becomes intense when the "beggar" says, "your lord is now at hand." Finally Eumaios asks who Odysseus is, and he is told a long, false story, though it does contain two factual details—going to Troy and seizing the mast in a shipwreck. Again Eumaios reveals a sour, disappointed side. He has been fooled by "news" of Odysseus before. He is sure his master died without glory at sea. Odysseus tries to lure him into a deal: Odysseus will get a new shirt and cloak if Odysseus shows up; Eumaios can have him thrown off a cliff if his story is a lie. Eumaios doesn't agree to the deal—how would it look if one day he offered the stranger hospitality, and the next day he dumped him off a cliff?

At supper Eumaios, a generous host, gives Odysseus the chine, or tenderloin. Then the "beggar" tests Eumaios' loyalty with a story of a freezing night at Troy. The "beggar" says Odysseus, through trickery, got him a cloak for the night. After hearing the story, Eumaios moves Odysseus' bed near the fire, puts more sheep and goat skins on it, and covers Odysseus with his own extra cloak. Then he wraps himself in a cloak and goes out to keep watch over his herds even though it is a rainy night. Odysseus rejoices to see Eumaios so faithful in his duties.

NOTE: In reading about Eumaios you may be reminded of some biblical themes: the faithful servant, the ideals of loyalty and obedience, the concept that there is a spiritual quality in all people, which in Homer takes the form of the idea that all must be treated well, for anyone may be a god in disguise.

BOOK 15: HOW THEY CAME TO ITHAKA

Athena comes to Telemakhos in Sparta (you have not seen him since Book 4). No slouch at making up stories herself, to spur him homeward she tells him Penelope is about to marry Eurymakhos. If she does, she will take all of Telemakhos' inheritance as her dowry, completely forgetting her first husband and the child of that husband. Because of the ambush, Telemakhos is to sail home at night east of the channel "between Ithaka and Same's rocky side," land alone, send the ship into port without him, and proceed on foot to the swineherd to spend the night.

The next day the swineherd should go to town and tell Penelope that Telemakhos is safely home. Telemakhos' gifts should be entrusted to a worthy person until such time as Telemakhos may marry. Watch for further references to Telemakhos and marriage. Marriage is for men and he is now being treated like a man. He is impatient to be off, and kicks Peisistratos awake. His friend wisely says they should wait until dawn, have a proper leave-taking, and receive gifts from Menelaos.

Telemakhos meets Menelaos in the hall and tells him that the "longing has come upon me to go home." Menelaos replies that he will not detain him unless, of course, Telemakhos might like to accompany Menelaos on a short tour. They would visit a few towns on his way back to his ship and could call on various noblemen and collect rich gifts. Just as Odysseus declined the offer of Nausikaa without ever coming out and saying no, Telemakhos declines this invitation by repeating his concern about affairs at home.

Peisistratos was right about the gifts. Menelaos gives Telemakhos a double-handled wine cup and a silver winebowl. Helen's gift is an embroidered robe "for his bride when that day comes." Imagine Telemakhos' feelings as "happily he took it." Helen is the most beautiful woman in the world. Do you think she would give Telemakhos such a gift if she, herself, did not find him attractive as a man? After breakfast the young men drive the chariot out of the gateway in the walled courtyard. Outside, Menelaos makes a libation, says farewell, and sends greetings to Nestor.

When Telemakhos wishes Odysseus were at Ithaka to see all the gifts Menelaos has bestowed on him, an omen appears: an eagle snags a white goose in its talons. Peisistratos asks Menelaos to interpret the omen. While the hero "of the great war cry," the "clarion in battle," gropes for words, Helen says Odysseus is the eagle and the suitors are the goose. You, of course, know Odysseus is in Ithaka right now, though nobody else does. Compare Telemakhos' good-bye to Helen with Odysseus' good-bye to Nausikaa. Are these standard polite phrases, or is Homer suggesting a real similarity between father and son?

The solidity of the friendship between Peisistratos and Telemakhos shows in Telemakhos' request to be taken straight to his ship, avoiding an overnight visit with Nestor. Peisistratos is loyal to his friend, rather than to his father. The arrival of Theoklymenos may remind you of the interrupted narrative in Book 2, when old Aigyptos spoke at the beginning of the assembly. Homer gives a lengthy pedigree for Theoklymenos and lets him tell his story. If you go back to your first glimpse of Telemakhos in Book 1, "sitting there, unhappy among the suitors, a boy, daydreaming," you will see how much Telemakhos has changed. He can even take on a hunted man now. In this interaction notice how he performs a number of small but decisive acts.

Back in Ithaka Odysseus tests Eumaios again by offering to leave, but his host invites him to remain. The narrative is interrupted again, and slowed down again, when Eumaios tells his life story. While Odysseus and the swineherd talk all night, Telemakhos lands in secret. Theoklymenos says another omen, a hawk's attack on a dove, means that the family of Telemakhos will rule in Ithaka forever. Telemakhos entrusts his gifts to his shipmate, Peiraios, and proceeds as instructed on foot to the swineherd's.

BOOK 16: FATHER AND SON

Book 16 begins dramatically. While Eumaios and Odysseus breakfast, Odysseus hears footsteps and notices that the dogs don't bark. When Telemakhos appears, Eumaios, in his surprise, drops a bowl and jug, then kisses Telemakhos' head, eyes, and hands, like a father in tears welcoming a returning son. The irony is heavy. Try to visualize all the small but significant acts of courtesy that occur after Telemakhos enters the hut. Every bit of dialogue, every act, is fraught with meaning because Odysseus is present, in disguise.

When Eumaios tells Telemakhos that the "guest" craves Telemakhos' protection, Telemakhos seems quite different from the way he was when he offered his help to Theoklymenos. He's back in Ithaka and all the problems are still here. He feels weak, untrained, unable to defend himself. When Odysseus says it's better to die fighting than to do nothing, Telemakhos explains that the matter of the suitors is in the hands of the gods, for although there is no bad feeling in the town against him, he is alone—without brothers—and his mother is powerless.

As soon as Eumaios goes off to tell Penelope that Telemakhos is safely back, Athena instructs Odysseus to reveal himself to his son. Turn back to the description of the "beggar" at the end of Book 13 and compare it to the glowing picture here. Also notice how Telemakhos reacts, first thinking Odysseus must be a god, then suspecting a trick on the part of the gods.

After a tearful reunion Odysseus and Telemakhos begin to lay their plans. Telemakhos, cautious, thinks the situation might defeat even Odysseus, but Odysseus, a true epic hero, has faith in Zeus and Athena. Telemakhos must learn to trust the gods, which may be the same as trusting his own best instincts.

Odysseus tells Telemakhos to go home and mingle with the suitors. When Odysseus disguised as the beggar arrives and is insulted, Telemakhos must not react. When Athena signals Odysseus, Odysseus will signal Telemakhos to hide the weapons in the storeroom. The excuses he is to offer to the suitors seem pretty flimsy, but as you have observed before, the suitors are blinded by their arrogance and greed.

NOTE: It's satisfying to see Telemakhos disagree with his father in the matter of checking the loyalty of the servants, a plan Odysseus originally proposes. Telemakhos says that can wait until later. You would not respect Telemakhos if after his successful foray into the world he simply agreed to every idea of his father's without a murmur.

In the meantime, Telemakhos' ship has arrived, and Penelope gets the news of her son's return. After hauling the ambush ship on shore, the suitors meet in private assembly. Antinoos, who headed the ambush, seems angry that his quarry gave him the slip, and wants to kill Telemakhos in some remote place, then lay claim to his stores and livestock. But Amphinomos, probably the least inherently evil of the group, thinks the murder is not right and that the suitors should consult the gods. He prevails, and although of course the gods are not consulted, the suitors return to Odysseus' house.

At this point in the story Penelope, who has heard (again from Medon) that the suitors may be plotting the death of her son in his own house, decides to appear before them, perhaps to distract them from her child, mostly to vent her anger and frustration. Currying favor with her, Eurymakhos promises to protect Telemakhos, though Homer tells us that Eurymakhos' speech is all lies. Penelope retreats upstairs and weeps for her husband until Athena soothes her to sleep.

NOTE: Penelope has the beauty, wit, and wealth to attract suitors not only from Ithaka but from neighboring islands. But she has no power, only the traditional female ploys of delay and deception, as symbolized in her weaving and unweaving of the shroud. Klytaimnestra's alliance with Agisthos becomes more understandable when you think about Penelope's plight. Penelope's holding out for twenty years, against all the evidence, for her husband to return has its epic proportions, too.

Before Eumaios returns to his hut, Athena changes Odysseus back into a beggar. He will suffer humiliations before he is raised to glory. Eumaios reports that Penelope knows of Telemakhos' return, and that the ambush ship is apparently back. The three together cook, eat, and sleep: father, son, and faithful servant.

BOOK 17: THE BEGGAR AT THE MANOR

The action now picks up steam. First, Telemakhos goes home to see his mother. She greets him as "Telemakhos, more sweet to me than sunlight!" Though she wants to hear his news, he delays, sending her to pray for revenge on the suitors. She is a "good woman" of this era, and does what she's told.

In town Telemakhos sees Mentor and two other old friends of his father, Antiphos and Halitherses. Peiraios tells Telemakhos he must collect his gifts from Menelaos, but Telemakhos leaves them where they are—Peiraios will have them if Telemakhos is killed. These arrangements let you know that Telemakhos is aware that he is going into his first battle, and may not survive it.

Telemakhos takes Theoklymenos home—an important guest because of his gift of prophecy. After the rituals of bathing and eating, Penelope asks a second time for Telemakhos' news and this time she gets it. He recaps his visits with Nestor and Menelaos, and adds the information that Odysseus is being detained by Kalypso. This report makes Penelope's "heart stir in her breast," but before she can speak Theoklymenos says this news is no longer valid, for the omen has told him that Odysseus is here, now, in Ithaka. Penelope's response is cautious: if that were so, Theoklymenos would be rewarded with many gifts. Apparently she's not about to believe him; she's heard many rumors for many years.

In the meantime the suitors, who have been throwing the discus and javelin (today they'd be tossing around a football), are called to dinner by Medon, the crier. While they start to feast, Eumaios and Odysseus disguised as the beggar head toward town. On the way the goatherd, Melanthios, insults Odysseus and kicks him. He serves as a strong contrast to Eumaios, the faithful servant.

NOTE: The house of Odysseus, like the other great houses in the story, is built around a large walled courtyard floored with hard packed earth. Armor and weapons hang on the walls. The women's hall is upstairs overlooking the courtyard.

As Odysseus and Eumaios approach, they agree that Eumaios will enter first, alone. While they discuss their approach, Odysseus notices his old dog Argos, lying on a pile of dung before the gate. Argos recognizes his master and tries to wag his tail, then dies, free to die now that his true master is at home. The incident emphasizes the theme of loyalty.

Watch the interplay of personalities carefully once Odysseus has entered the courtyard. Barbarians are hostile to strangers (have you ever been the new kid in a strange school?). Civilized people like the Akhaians are supposed to be hospitable. You'll see that Antinoos seems even more insolent than before, when he throws a stool at Odysseus. Another omen occurs when Telemakhos sneezes and his mother laughs, taking the sneeze as a good sign. It's pleasant to hear her laugh, since up until now she's been most-

ly angry, frustrated, and sad. She wants to question
the beggar, but he doesn't wish to rile the already
rowdy suitors—he will come to her later. Homer
builds the suspense about this meeting between husband and wife by postponing it, and makes it more
dramatic by having it occur after dark. Eumaios, ever
true to his job, leaves to tend his pigs, though he will
return in the morning with animals for slaughter. The
chapter ends with food, dance, and song as the day
wanes to evening.

BOOK 18: BLOWS AND A QUEEN'S BEAUTY

In the midst of the festivities Iros, a real beggar,
appears. He has begging privileges here and resents
seeing Odysseus on his turf. The suitors egg him into
a boxing match. They're impressed with Odysseus'
physique when he strips to fight. "By god, old Iros
now retiros," one of them quips, seeing Odysseus'
muscles. As usual Odysseus considers two courses of
action: to kill Iros with one blow, or to be more gentle.
His "gentle" punch shatters Iros' jaw and knocks out
his teeth. So Odysseus, ironically enough, but useful-
ly for his purposes, takes over as "official" beggar to
the suitors.

NOTE: Now the storyteller's foreknowledge adds
grimness to the tale. Amphinomos has been depicted
as one of the better suitors. He's generous to Odysseus here, is "gently bred," an "easy man." Odysseus
warns him that the suitors' impiety will be punished,
and that he should leave. But you are told Athena has

Amphinomos marked to stay and that he will be killed by a spear thrown by Telemakhos. A man's fate is inevitable.

In these latter chapters you finally see more of Penelope. Athena, wanting to fan the suitors' desire and show off Penelope's beauty before her husband and son, puts it into her head to appear before the company. Penelope laughs confusedly and doesn't quite know why she's doing what she's doing. She refuses to bathe and adorn herself, but Athena puts her into a beauty sleep from which she wakes looking her best. She appears, veiled, with two of her maids, and the suitors show their pleasure. First she speaks only to her son, but then, bolder, she tells the suitors that her husband instructed her when he left to wait for his return until the beard appeared on their son's cheek. She implies the time has come, chides them for not bringing her gifts of courtship, and uses their desire for her to make them give her jewels and a dress. Odysseus secretly enjoys seeing her entice them into giving her presents. She's not helpless and obedient in this scene. She's strong and clever.

After Penelope withdraws, the suitors give themselves up to dance and song. You learn more about the various alliances of the suitors when Melantho speaks insultingly to Odysseus. She's the mistress of Eurymakhos, a fact that makes his admiration of Penelope's "deep-minded beauty" sound a bit thin. Eurymakhos taunts Odysseus about his baldness, and throws a stool at him. Athena, it seems, wants Odysseus mortified still more, wishes to test his patience to the utmost. Again Amphinomos shows himself a reasonable fellow by calming the quarreling suitors and advising them to go to bed.

BOOK 19: RECOGNITIONS AND A DREAM

With the suitors safely bedded, Telemakhos and Odysseus lock the weapons and armor in the storeroom. Then Telemakhos goes to bed. Odysseus receives another insult from Melantho. Eurynome, the housekeeper, spreads a couch for Odysseus and finally he and Penelope sit down to talk in private. "Who are you, where do you come from?" she asks. He doesn't explain right away. She tells of her situation, the trick of the shroud, and says, "I have no strength left to evade a marriage." It's an intimate conversation for a woman of her rank to be having with a beggar. She asks him about himself again, and this time he tells her a false story, again saying he's from Krete. You might compare this version with the one he told Eumaios in Book 14. He says he once entertained Odysseus at Knossos, and when Penelope weeps for her lord "like melting mountain snow," you're told that he weeps inwardly, that he has the ability to hide his feelings.

When she asks for proof that he really knew Odysseus, he describes his own clothes of twenty years ago: cloak, pin, shirt, also his woolly-headed herald, Eurybates. She is strangely moved, and cries again. She believes him. This whole scene is highly charged emotionally, so much so that some critics argue that Penelope may unconsciously know she is speaking to her husband.

He says he's heard that Odysseus has made a fortune among the Thesprotians. He adds a bit of factual material about the Phaiakians—perhaps even Odysseus, the master of self-control, is having a hard time concealing how he really feels and is skating dangerously close to telling her the truth. He says that even now Odysseus is on a ship, wealthy, close to home—in fact, he will be there tomorrow! Here Penelope backs away, as she did when Theoklymenos said Odysseus was at hand. The details of his clothing are tangible proof to her. An assertion, out of nowhere, that her husband is almost there is less convincing. But she does feel strongly about this stranger.

She calls for a bed to be made for him, and mentions a bath. He refuses a footbath unless it is given by an old woman, someone like himself in years. He is staying in his character of an elderly beggar. Calling Eurykleia, Penelope stops herself from saying, "Come bathe your master's feet." Homer keeps you on the edge of your chair all through this scene. Will the secret of Odysseus' identity be revealed? Or will it remain hidden?

By insisting on an old maidservant like Eurykleia, Odysseus has almost asked to be recognized, for Eurykleia nursed him as a baby and knows him inside and out. She feels Odysseus' presence even before she starts to bathe his feet. She tells him many strangers have come but none who seemed so like Odysseus as he does. But Homer delays the moment of revelation in a masterful way. First, he has Odysseus remember the scar on his thigh, worry that Eurykleia will notice it, and tell us the story of how he got it. This digression takes quite a while and is full of interesting details, all of them just as interesting, Homer seems to imply, as what is about to happen. But when you return to what *is* about to happen, it's even more dramatic because you had to wait for it. Eurykleia sees the scar. *"You are Odysseus!"* she exclaims. She has no doubt. It's a moment of intense feeling for her, for Odysseus, and for the reader. Odysseus swears her to secrecy, and Athena distracts Penelope from noticing.

But this powerful chapter has not yet reached its climax. Bedtime approaches. Penelope tells the stranger how hard the nights are for her, alone, tortured by her situation, not knowing what to do. Imagine how those words must affect Odysseus. Telemakhos is no longer a boy, she says. (He proved that in Books 1–4.) She's going to have to do something. She asks the stranger to interpret a dream of an eagle attacking twenty fat geese. The eagle spoke to her and said he was Odysseus. The stranger says it is a true dream and that Odysseus has shown her the doom of the suitors. She speaks of true and false dreams for a bit, but then, almost as though she were bringing to consciousness an unconsciously arrived at decision, she tells the stranger she has decided to act. Tomorrow she will present the suitors with her husband's bow and challenge them to string it and shoot it straight through twelve axe heads as only her husband was able to do. The man who performs this feat will have her hand. She could have decided to do this a week from now, or even a year from now, but something—perhaps her unconscious awareness of her husband's presence—makes her decide to do it tomorrow.

Let there be no delay of the trial, the stranger says, Odysseus will be there. It's wrenching as the scene ends to see Penelope go up to bed alone. It's hard not to feel that on some level she believes that Odysseus *will* be there, that perhaps he has even been there already.

BOOK 20: SIGNS AND A VISION

This book opens with Odysseus lying in the entryway on an oxhide and fleeces, under a robe Eurynome has thrown over him. Epic hero though he is, he can't sleep. He's keyed up, thinking of the undoing of his enemies. He almost loses his self-control when he sees the corrupt maids sneaking out of the house to sleep with the suitors (perhaps he is also reminded of his wife sleeping alone upstairs). Homer describes him rocking from side to side, filled with anger, trying to keep his temper. Anyone who has ever physically struggled to keep from exploding can identify with him. Finally Athena (his good sense) comes to him and he sleeps.

Upstairs, Penelope, too, is wakeful. Having decided at last to let the suitors compete for her hand, she is miserable and prays for death. Her anguish is more painful because today she thought she saw Odysseus as she remembered him, real, not in a dream. Homer tells us that Odysseus hears her cry out and that she seems to stand by him and recognize him.

It's morning. Odysseus goes outdoors and prays for a sign from Zeus, who sends a thunderbolt. The weakest of twelve maids grinding corn hears it and prays for the suitors' destruction.

There are morning chores to be done. Odysseus is insulted again by Melanthios, the goatherd. Compare him to the new character, Philoitios, the cattle foreman, who arrives with an ox and goats for the suitors. Odysseus sees immediately that Philoitios is a good fighter and loyal servant, and tells him Odysseus is coming soon.

A sign from the gods prevents the suitors from trying again to kill Telemakhos: an eagle with a rock dove in its claws. Amphinomos says this omen is unlucky for their plan. They decide to have breakfast. Telemakhos serves Odysseus food and restrains the suitors' rowdiness, but Athena wants Odysseus to taste more gall before his hour of triumph. Ktesippos throws a cow's foot at him. Telemakhos blazes up at the men,

telling them to curb their viciousness. The suitor Agelaos tells Telemakhos to go to his mother and insist
that she make a decision so Telemakhos can keep his
inheritance while she becomes a new wife in a new
house. Telemakhos replies that he can't make his
mother marry against her will. A chilling moment follows. Athena makes the suitors laugh uncontrollably,
wheeze, neigh, and cry. Blood defiles the meat they
eat.

Theoklymenos, the visionary, sees blood running
down the walls and ghosts crowding the courtyard
and entryway. The suitors laugh at him. Eurymakhos
says he has lost his mind, but Theoklymenos
declaims: "Damnation and black night I see arriving."
He leaves this evil place and goes to stay with Peiraios. The suitors ridicule Telemakhos for bringing
home the hungry beggar and this crazy Theoklymenos with his foolish prophecies. Their meal continues,
but it is a cold feast.

BOOK 21: THE TEST OF THE BOW

NOTE: Scholars believe that this part of the story,
the trial of the great crossbow, goes back to its earliest
origins. Performing a feat to win a woman's hand is
basic to some of our oldest folk and fairy tales.

Penelope gets the bow from the storeroom, and
Homer can't resist telling us how Odysseus came to
have the bow. She brings a quiver of arrows "spiked
with coughing death." Her maids bring a basket of
axe heads, and she makes her announcement. The
swineherd and cowherd are moved to tears by the
sight of the bow, which angers Antinoos. He makes
fun of them, accepts the challenge of the bow as fair,
saying he remembers Odysseus from childhood.

Another moment of grim foreshadowing occurs as
Homer says that Antinoos will be Odysseus' first victim.

Earlier Odysseus showed the emotional stress he
was under by rocking from side to side. Here Telemakhos reacts to the strain by snorting with laughter.
He, too, is keyed up and nervous, perhaps also aware
of the irony in Antinoos' remembering Odysseus,
who after all is standing right there. Telemakhos digs
a trench and sets the axe heads in a row.

NOTE: For years scholars have puzzled about
exactly how he does it. Robert Fitzgerald thinks the
axes have double heads, so one blade is buried in
earth and the target is the twelve socket holes. Denys
Page, in his book on folktales (listed in the Further
Reading section), suggests that the axes are ceremoni-
al, with bronze or iron handles from which they cus-
tomarily hang, by rings in the ends of the handles.
Page thinks the target is the twelve holes in the ends
of the handles.

Telemakhos tries three times to string the bow and
almost does it on the fourth try, when "a stiffening in
Odysseus made him check." Have you ever been
wrestling or running or swimming with your father
and suddenly realized you could beat him, but you
held back? It's a bit overwhelming to discover that
you're as strong or stronger than your father. Now
Leodes tries the bow and fails. Antinoos, directing the
proceedings, orders Melanthios to light a fire and get
some lard. They'll heat and grease the bow to try to
limber it up. More suitors try and fail.

In the meantime the swineherd and cowherd leave
the hall, downcast. Odysseus slips outside to speak
with them. He asks if they would stand beside Odys-

seus in a fight, and when he is assured that they
would, he tells them who he is. Their joy is cut short
as he gives them orders. He says the suitors won't
want him to try the bow, but Eumaios must defy them
and bring it to him. Eumaios must tell the women to
lock their door and stay inside their hall, no matter
what they hear going on in the courtyard. Philoitios
must run on the signal to the outer gate, lock it, and
lash it shut. The suitors will soon find themselves
weaponless and trapped.

The three return to the courtyard, where Eurymakhos takes his time with the bow: "He turned it round,
and turned it round before the licking flame to warm
it up." But he can't string it, and the humiliation
stings. He says the suitors are like children compared
to Odysseus. He feels ashamed. Antinoos is the last
suitor, the strongest, the one with the best chance.
But apparently he is daunted by the idea of failure, for
at this point he suddenly says they should postpone
further trials of the bow. You never find out if he
could have done it, for he doesn't even try.

Now Odysseus says he would like to try. Antinoos,
angry, says he must be drunk. Eurymakhos says it
would be terrible if this beggar succeeded and people
heard about it. Penelope says to let the beggar try. At
this point Telemakhos speaks sharply to his mother,
sending her upstairs, saying that he will decide who
gets to try the bow. He knows blood is about to be
shed and he wants his mother safely out of the
way.

Eumaios starts toward Odysseus with the bow. The
suitors raise an ugly din of protests, and Eumaios fal-
ters, setting the bow down. Telemakhos yells, "take
him the bow!" He rails at the suitors, and one of them
finds his frenzy amusing. That laughter sets off more
laughter and the tension is broken. If a riot broke out

here, Odysseus might never get a chance to try the bow.

But he does. (By now the women are shut in their hall and the courtyard gate is locked and lashed.) Odysseus takes his time, tapping the bow inch by inch looking for holes made by termites. The suitors mock him, calling him a bow lover, a dealer in old bows. Odysseus strings the bow in one motion and plucks the string, which sings a single note. The faces of the suitors change. Zeus thunders. Seated on a stool, Odysseus fits an arrow to the crossbow and makes the incredible shot. He says to Telemakhos, with heavy irony, "The hour has come to cook their lordships' mutton—supper by daylight." With sword and spear, Telemakhos moves to his father's side.

BOOK 22: DEATH IN THE GREAT HALL

Odysseus positions himself in front of the only doorway, pours the arrows out of the quiver into a pile at his feet, and shoots Antinoos. Antinoos is drinking with his head tipped back when he's hit: "Odysseus' arrow hit him under the chin and punched up to the feathers through his throat." "Did he dream of death?" Homer asks. "How could he?" Antinoos' nostrils spurt blood and in his death throes he kicks over his table, knocking his meat and bread to the ground "to soak in dusty blood." It's a graphic description, like those in *The Illiad*, where many deaths in battle are shown in similar detail.

The suitors think the shot that killed Antinoos was accidental. Not so. Odysseus reveals his identity and states their crimes against him. This is his moment. Anyone who has ever wished to get revenge on enemies can understand why the hero's adrenalin is starting to pump. The suitors hunt for an exit, and Eurymakhos tries to bargain with Odysseus, but Odysseus will not compromise. No one will escape. Eurymakhos rallies the suitors, telling them to grab their swords, and rush Odysseus. Eurymakhos attacks first, but Odysseus stops him with an arrow. Amphinomos comes running at him next. As predicted, Telemakhos kills him with a spear. It hurts to see Amphinomos die. Then Odysseus holds off the suitors while Telemakhos runs to the storeroom for armor and weapons. While the two servants and Telemakhos equip themselves, Odysseus keeps shooting. He does not waste one arrow.

The suitors are dwindling fast. Melanthios volunteers to climb the wall and fetch weapons from the storeroom. When Odysseus sees what's afoot, he sends the two servants to catch Melanthios and hang him from the storeroom rafters.

The four now face forty remaining men. Athena appears briefly to give them courage. She spurs Odysseus on, even taunts him, then disappears in the form of a swallow. Agelaos now leads the suitors, and his strategy is to get Odysseus. He has six of them aim at him at once, but Athena makes the shots miss. The four, however, throw their lances and kill four suitors, then rush to take the fallen men's spears while the suitors retreat. The suitors take aim and throw again, but Athena interferes once more, though just to make the fight seem fair, Homer tells us that Telemakhos gets a superficial wound on the wrist and Eumaios' shoulder gets grazed. Again the four successfully hurl their spears. The cowherd hits Ktesippos, the man who threw the cow's foot at Odysseus.

At this point the aegis, Athena's shield, appears aloft in the courtyard and terrifies the suitors, who begin to run wildly and beg for mercy. Odysseus kills

Leodes despite his pleas, but he sends Medon, the crier, and Phemios, the bard, outside to safety. All of the suitors now lie dead, like a pile of fish poured from a net. Odysseus sends for Eurykleia. When she sees him covered with blood, she begins to exult, but he stops her. "To glory over slain men is no piety," he says. He asks her to separate the righteous from the wicked maids. The corrupt ones are made to haul out the dead and scrub down the hall. Telemakhos and the cowherd scrape the earth with hoes, but the women have to carry out the blood-soaked mud. Then Telemakhos and the cowherd hang the twelve disloyal maids: "Their feet danced for a little, but not long."

Melanthios is brought from the storeroom and killed by mutilation. His nose, ears, genitals, hands and feet are cut off. The smoke from fire and burning brimstone (sulfur) are used to purify the courtyard. The four victors wash their bloody hands and feet. Eurykleia calls the loyal maids. The servants welcome Odysseus, kiss him, and cry. The chapter ends with the revenge complete.

BOOK 23: THE TRUNK OF THE OLIVE TREE

NOTE: Homer shows himself the master of variety, able to give a wide-ranging battle in one chapter and a subtle psychological study in the next. When Eurykleia calls Penelope to come and greet her husband, you might expect, if this were a TV soap opera, a moment of hesitation followed by a big clinch. Instead, Penelope, like her husband, is cautious and intelligent. She shows the power of that intelligence, the quality that makes her worth struggling to get home to for twenty rough years.

Penelope enters the courtyard but keeps her distance, still not convinced that this man is truly Odysseus. She sits down across the room from him and looks at him. He sits with eyes lowered and waits.

When Telemakhos chides her for her coldness, she says she is stunned. She cannot speak to him yet, cannot even keep her eyes on his face. Have you ever felt like this, so filled with doubt and longing that you could barely look at someone? She says if it is really Odysseus, they will know each other, for they have their secrets. At this, Odysseus smiles. "Peace," he says to Telemakhos. "Let your mother test me at her leisure." Imagine his state of mind. He is still in rags and covered with the blood of battle. He knows he has just killed the flower of Ithaka's manhood and will have to answer for it. He is probably even tired.

In order to deceive the townspeople into thinking all is well, Odysseus has the women dress up and the harper play for dancing. To passersby it will seem like a wedding is in progress within. Then Odysseus is bathed by Eurynome. Athena improves his looks, and he dresses in clean clothes. He returns to the same chair by the pillar, facing his silent wife across the room. Have you ever noticed that people feeling shy or doubtful like to sit or stand with their backs toward something solid, like a wall or large piece of furniture?

He says she is strange, hard. He says her heart is iron within her breast. "Strange woman," he calls her, and in reply she calls him, "Strange man." Still they sit apart. He waits, and she waits, and you wait. Homer knows all about suspense and how pleasure is heightened if it is delayed.

Now comes the test, though of course Penelope is too canny to announce it. She simply tells Eurykleia to make up the bed in the master bedroom and place it outside the chamber. Suddenly Odysseus has a reason to be angry. He built that bed. One of its posts is the trunk of an olive tree. The bed cannot be moved unless someone has sawed off that bedpost. Only husband and wife and Penelope's one slave know the secret of this bed—only husbands and wives know the secrets of their beds, Homer seems to be saying. The bedpost that is a rooted tree suggests the fidelity that makes the strong bond between these two. This is the final proof that convinces Penelope of Odysseus' identity. They embrace at last. In Odysseus' arms, Penelope is as longed for as the sun-warmed earth is longed for by an exhausted swimmer. Anyone who has swum to the point of being bone cold and worn out and then settled on the hot beach knows what Homer is talking about: warmth, safety, relief.

Like any long-separated couple, now they talk. He says they are not yet in the clear. He wants to take her to bed, but she first wants to hear about the last journey Teiresias foretold for him. "My strange one," he calls her, but he tells her Teiresias' prophesy. She says that though the gods have robbed them of their best years together, at least their age may be kind. Eurynome and Eurykleia make the bed for them. Telemakhos hushes the dancing and the women in the courtyard. The ruse of the "wedding" seems to come true, as husband and wife "mingle in love."

At dawn the realities must be faced. Odysseus, Telemakhos, and the two herdsmen leave quickly for the country, to see Odysseus' aged father, Laertes, and to plan how they will deal with the anger of the town when the deaths of the suitors are known.

BOOK 24: WARRIORS, FAREWELL

NOTE: The pace changes again. Instead of staying with Odysseus, Homer shifts the scene to Hades
where the dead suitors are arriving, squeaking like
bats.

The suitors are no longer interesting, not compared
to the heroes Akhilleus and Agamemnon whose
ghosts are also in Hades. Akhilleus tells Agamemnon
that he should have had a glorious death at Troy,
whereupon Agamemnon describes Akhilleus' own
funeral to him. It was quite an occasion, what with his
goddess mother's arrival, the funeral pyre, the min-
gling of his bones with those of his best friend, Patroklos, the heaped-up tomb, and funeral games. Its
pomp and glory contrast with Agamemnon's ignominious ending. Without saying it directly, Homer
makes you aware that Odysseus could have had
either of these two fates. But after a stormy period
from roughly ages twenty-five to forty-five, he has
been chosen to live to a serene old age, knowing
domestic happiness and kingly peace. Agamemnon is
not petty about his friend's good fortune. When he
questions one of the suitors and hears about Odysseus' homecoming, he is jubilant that Penelope was
faithful and that Odysseus succeeded where he
failed.

In the meantime Odysseus and his friends reach
the country. While the others have breakfast at a farmhouse, Odysseus goes to find his father. Laertes is
dressed in workman's clothes, cultivating the earth
around a young fruit tree. Should Odysseus run to
him or test him first? By now you know Odysseus
well enough to predict what he will do. As usual he

tells a false story, in which he claims to have met Odysseus. But when he sees his suffering father put a handful of dust on his head as a sign of grief and despair, he can hold back no longer and tells Laertes who he is. His scar is one proof, but a stronger proof is his memory of the precise number of pear, apple, and fig trees that Laertes planted for him years ago. Knowing his son at last, Laertes nearly faints and clutches Odysseus for support.

Laertes worries that the Ithakans will want revenge for the deaths of the suitors. Back at the farmhouse Laertes is bathed and dressed in new clothes more suitable for his rank. Athena makes him look young and vigorous.

While the people at the farmhouse eat at midday (Homer keeps careful track of meals), the relatives of the suitors hold an assembly. The father of Antinoos, Eupeithes, wants a bloody revenge. Medon tells the citizens that Odysseus was aided by a god. Halitherses, Odysseus' old friend, says, "You would not control your sons," you brought this on yourselves. Observing from Mount Olympos, Athena asks Zeus if this discord will go on forever. It could. Wars lasting generations have started over less. But Zeus wants this quarrel to end. Odysseus' honor is satisfied. He will be king by a pact sworn forever, and the gods will blot out the memory of the slain sons and brothers.

So Athena goes to the farmhouse to warn Odysseus. As the angry crowd approaches, Odysseus challenges Telemakhos to manly fighting, and Telemakhos says, in effect, "Let me at 'em." He's no longer the wistful boy you saw in Book 1. Laertes delights at hearing his son and grandson spar with each other.

As the citizens appear, Athena urges Laertes to throw his spear, killing Eupeithes. Odysseus and his men attack, and more blood would have been spilled had Athena not stopped the fight. When she appears before them, the townspeople flee. Odysseus is about to pursue them when Zeus throws a thunderbolt: No more. Later a peace pact is sworn to by all parties, under the guidance of Athena.

A STEP BEYOND

Tests and Answers
TESTS

Test 1

1. The first appearance of Odysseus in *The Odyssey* finds him
   A. in the court of the Phoenicians
   B. in Ithaka
   C. on Kalypso's island

2. The god who is least inclined to assist Odysseus on the latter's homeward journey is
   A. Poseidon   B. Zeus   C. Hermes

3. Telemakhos sets out to
   A. seek Athena's help
   B. find his father
   C. make peace with the suitors

4. The saying that best illustrates Odysseus' adventure with Skylla and Kharybdis is
   A. "All's well that ends well"
   B. "Out of the frying pan, into the fire"
   C. "The grass is always greener on the other side of the fence"

5. Odysseus weeps when he hears a minstrel sing of
   A. Poseidon's wrath
   B. Akhilleus' death
   C. Telemakhos' birth

6. Teiresias is   _____
   A. a minor god   B. a blind prophet
   C. the keeper of the gate to the underworld

7. Eurykleia recognizes Odysseus by   _____
   A. a scar   B. his clothes   C. a birthmark

8. What Kirke and the Seirenes have in common   _____
   is that they
   A. can change the form of men
   B. tempt and destroy men
   C. befriend Odysseus

9. Nausikaa is   _____
   A. Odysseus' dog   B. a beautiful princess
   C. Odysseus' childhood nurse

10. Of the following, the one whose life is spared _____
    by Odysseus is
    A. Antinoos   B. Phemios   C. Melanthios

11. Describe Homer's narrative technique or storytelling
    style, giving five examples from *The Oddyssey*.

12. Discuss Telemakhos as a developing character.

13. Analyze the personality of Odysseus as portrayed by
    Homer, giving three examples from *The Odyssey*.

14. Discuss the triumph of good over evil in *The Odyssey*.

Test 2

1. It is prophesied that Odysseus will die   _____
   A. in Ithaka   B. on a mountaintop   C. at sea

2. The phrase that best describes Odysseus is   _____
   A. "quiet and unassuming"
   B. "unfailingly honest"
   C. "dangerously arrogant"

3. Odysseus is carried from the Kyklopes' cave   _____
   by a
   A. ram   B. sheep   C. donkey

4. Polyphemos' father is _____
   A. Poseidon   B. Zeus   C. Hades

5. Which does Eurylokhos not do? _____
   A. lead half of Odysseus' men in search of Kirke
   B. encourage Odysseus' men to eat forbidden cattle
   C. save several of Odysseus' men from death at the hands of Polyphemos

6. Telemakhos and Odysseus meet in _____
   A. Athens
   B. a swineherd's hut
   C. Odysseus' old room

7. When Odysseus is recognized by his dog, the animal _____
   A. gives his master away
   B. runs from the room
   C. dies

8. The god of the winds gives Odysseus a(n) _____
   A. sack full of wind   B. basket of food
   C. amulet which controls the weather

9. Shakespeare's observation that "All that glistens is not gold" best applies to the adventure of Odysseus' men and _____
   A. the lotus-eaters   B. Skylla and Kharybdis
   C. the Kyklopes

10. The battle that is about to erupt in the final book of The Odyssey is stopped by _____
    A. the pleas of Odysseus   B. a sign from Zeus
    C. the prayers of Penelope

11. Define fate as that concept appears in The Odyssey, giving three examples.

12. Describe the heroic code that underlies the concepts of right behavior in The Odyssey.

13. Discuss Odysseus in relation to the female characters he encounters in *The Odyssey*.

14. Discuss the roles of five minor characters in developing the themes of *The Odyssey*.

ANSWERS

Test 1

1. C   **2.** A   **3.** B   **4.** B   **5.** B   **6.** B

7. A   **8.** B   **9.** B   **10.** B

11.   Here are five narrative techniques to discuss:

1. The story begins *in medias res*, in the middle of things.

2. The use of *flashbacks* such as when Odysseus recalls his wanderings.

3. The use of dramatic irony, such as when Odysseus returns home in disguise.

4. The use of epithets ("red-haired Menelaos") and epic similes for vividness and characterization, and as a breather for the oral storyteller.

5. The use of repetition, as in the story of Agamemnon.

12.   In Book 1 Telemakhos is powerless, boyish, wistful, passive: "sitting there, unhappy among the suitors, a boy, daydreaming." The assembly of citizens will not back him against the suitors.

On his travels Telemakhos gains information about his father, and esteem and rich gifts from Nestor and Menelaos. Helen affirms his manhood with her gift of a marriage robe. He makes Peisistratos his friend, avoids ambush, and returns to fight bravely against the suitors at his father's side.

13.   Here is an outline of Odysseus' qualities, which you can develop with examples from the poem.

1. Loyalty: his yearning to return home even after eight years with Kalypso.

2. Intelligence: quick wit (inside the Trojan horse, inside the Kyklopes' cave); invention of stories (to his father, to Eumaios); perceptiveness about people (in approaching Nausikaa and Penelope).

3. Valor: in combatting the Kyklopes, the force of the ocean, the suitors.

14. Here are examples of the triumph of good over evil, which you can work into your essay:

1. Telemakhos overcomes his weakness and passivity.

2. Penelope, through ruse, postpones a decision and thus keeps the greed and arrogance of the suitors in check.

3. Odysseus conquers all obstacles and reasserts himself in Ithaka, restoring the virtues of loyalty and respect for the gods as well as rightful kingship and domestic order.

Test 2

1. C   2. C   3. A   4. A   5. C   6. B
7. C   8. A   9. A   10. B

11. Fate is that which the gods have in store for men and which cannot be avoided. It is not necessarily related to a person's inherent virtue. Here are three examples of the working of fate.

1. Agamemnon's fate was to be murdered by his wife on his return from Troy. Odysseus' fate was to find a faithful wife and to win over the suitors.

2. Eating the cattle of the sun god is forbidden. The men know this, but eat them anyway. All perish but Odysseus, as was foretold by Teiresias.

3. Amphinomos, though decent, cannot avoid death in the final slaughter. Telemakhos kills him.

12. Valor, respect for the gods, intelligence and loyalty are all aspects of the heroic code. Odysseus' actions exemplify it best, but Nestor, Menelaos, and Telemakhos exhibit these qualities as well, and provide an echo of the hero's behavior.

13. Here are the female characters Odysseus encounters:

1. Kalypso. He is diplomatic about continuing to sleep with her and tactful about his departure.

2. Kirke. He is masterful in subduing her evil powers, and responsive to her invitation to his bed.

3. Nausikaa. He is delicate in approaching her, and protective in keeping her from embarrassment before her father.

4. Penelope. He is sensitive to her feelings in the matter of Eurykleia, and patient and perceptive during the reunion scene.

14. Here are five major themes and five minor characters who help develop these themes:

1. fate: Eurymakhos leads the men to slaughter the cattle of the sun god.

2. loyalty: Eurykleia dedicates her life to service.

3. hospitality: Eumaios is hospitable to the "beggar."

4. intelligence: Helen interprets the omen and penetrates Odysseus' disguise in Troy.

5. valor and vengeance: The cowherd kills Ktesippos.

Term Paper Ideas

1. Compare the Homeric epic hero with an example of today's antihero.

2. Discuss the role of humiliation in the making of a hero, with reference to *The Odyssey*.

3. Contrast a realistic, descriptive passage in *The Odyssey* with an idealized, descriptive passage as the basis for commenting on realistic versus idealistic writing.

4. Does Penelope unconsciously recognize Odysseus in Book 19?

5. Discuss the position of women in the Homeric world.

6. Examine the relationship between man and nature in *The Odyssey*.

7. Discuss ritual in *The Odyssey* as it applies to bathing, eating, and the sacrifice of animals.

8. Compare the themes of *The Iliad* and *The Odyssey*.

9. What aspects of political and social life in Homeric and pre-Homeric times are reflected in *The Odyssey*?

10. Compare the tests faced by Telemakhos with those faced by Odysseus.

11. Discuss the function of the Agamemnon story in *The Odyssey*.

12. Compare the heroes in *The Iliad* to Odysseus. How is Odysseus different from a traditional epic hero?

13. Discuss three events in *The Odyssey* that reveal three contradictory aspects of Odysseus' character.

14. Discuss the meaning of the Seirenes, Skylla and Kharybdis, and Aeolus.

15. Discuss the trial of the bow and axes as part of folkloric tradition.

16. Comment on Homer's style: his formal rhetoric, his use of sensory imagery, his occasional revelation of feeling.

17. Discuss Homer's use of irony in *The Odyssey*.

18. Where does the dramatic climax of *The Odyssey* come?

19. Comment on the role of Athena in *The Odyssey*. Defend the argument that she, not Penelope, is the leading female figure.

20. What is known about Homer's life and work? What is known about the oral tradition he is a part of? Why are his poems considered classics?

21. Discuss the relationship between Knossos, Troy, and Mycenae and *The Odyssey*.

84

Further Reading

Beye, Charles Rowan. The "Iliad," the "Odyssey" and the Epic Tradition. Garden City, N.Y.: Doubleday, 1966.

Bradford, Ernle. Ulysses Found. London: Hodder and Stoughton, 1963. A re-creation of the journey with photos and map.

Carpenter, Rhys. Folk Tale, Fiction and Saga in the Homeric Epics. Berkeley: University of California Press, 1958.

Clarke, Howard W. The Art of the Odyssey. Englewood Cliffs, N.J.: Prentice-Hall, 1967.

Cook, Albert, ed. "The Odyssey," a Norton Critical Edition. New York: W. W. Norton, 1974. Map and samples of reactions to The Odyssey in antiquity.

Finley, M. I. The World of Odysseus, 2d ed. London: Penguin, 1979.

Graves, Robert. Homer's Daughter. New York: Pyramid, 1955. A novel.

Greene, Thomas. The Descent from Heaven, a Study in Epic Continuity. New Haven: Yale University Press, 1963.

Kazantzakis, Nikos. Odyssey: A Modern Sequel. New York: Simon and Schuster, 1961.

Kirk, G. S. Homer and the Epic. Cambridge: Cambridge University Press, 1979.

Kitto, H. D. F. The Greeks. London: Penguin, 1957.

Lord, Albert B. The Singer of Tales. New York: Atheneum, 1971.

Page, Denys. Folktales in Homer's "Odyssey." Cambridge, Mass.: Harvard University Press, 1973.

Stanford, William B. The Ulysses Theme. Oxford: Blackwell, 1963.

Steiner, George, and Robert Fagles, eds. Homer, A Collection of Critical Essays. Englewood Cliffs, N.J.: Prentice-Hall, 1962.

Taylor, Charles H., Jr., ed. Essays on the "Odyssey." Bloomington: Indiana University Press, 1966.

Glossary

Agamemnon King of Mycenae; Greek leader at Troy, murdered by his wife Klytaimnestra on his return home; brother of Menelaos.

Agelaos One of the suitors of Penelope.

Aiaia Kirke's island.

Aias Greek hero at Troy, drowned on the return trip after defying the gods. Name also spelled Ajax.

Aigisthos Klytaimnestra's lover; usurper of Agamemnon's throne at Mycenae.

Aiolos King of the winds.

Akhaians Homer's name for the Greeks (as opposed to the Trojans).

Akhilleus The greatest Greek warrior at Troy.

Alkinoos King of the Phaiakians, host to Odysseus; father of Nausikaa, husband of Arete.

Amphinomes A suitor of Penelope.

Antinoos Ringleader of Penelope's suitors.

Arete Queen of the Phaiakians.

Athena Goddess of the arts and wisdom; patron of Odysseus.

Death Homer's name for Hades, ruler of the underworld.

Elpenor One of Odysseus' crew, dies when he falls off Kirke's roof.

Erebos The dark land of the dead.

Eumaios Faithful swineherd of Odysseus.

Eupeithes Father of Antinoos; killed by Laertes.

Eurykleia Old and faithful maidservant to Odysseus.

Eurylokhos Righthand man to Odysseus during his travels.

Eurymakhos Oily-tongued suitor to Penelope.

Eurynome Housekeeper to Penelope.

Hades   God of the underworld, Death.

Halitherses   Old friend of Odysseus in Ithaka.

Helen   Wife of Menelaos; carried off to Troy by Paris, causing the Trojan War.

Helios   Sun god whose sacred cattle are eaten by Odysseus' crew.

Hera   Queen of the gods, wife of Zeus.

Hermes   Messenger of the gods.

Ilium   Troy.

Iros   "Official" beggar to Penelope's suitors.

Ithaka   Island home of Odysseus.

Kalypso   Nymph who detains Odysseus eight years at Ogygia island.

Kharybdis   Whirlpool.

Kikones   People at Ismaros, raided by Odysseus.

Kirke   Enchantress who can turn men into swine.

Klytaimnestra   Murderous wife of Agamemnon.

Ktesippos   One of Penelope's suitors; killed by the cowherd.

Kyklopes   One-eyed son of Poseidon, blinded and tricked by Odysseus.

Laertes   Father of Odysseus.

Laistrygonians   Hostile people who attack Odysseus and his men.

Medon   The crier, spared during the slaughter.

Melanthios   Disloyal goatherd to Odysseus.

Melantho   Brazen maidservant to Odysseus.

Menelaos   Brother of Agamemnon, husband of Helen, host to Telemakhos.

Mentes   Old friend of Odysseus; one of Athena's disguises.

Mentor   Old friend of Odysseus; adviser to Telemakhos; disguise of Athena.

Muses   The nine goddesses who inspire the arts.

Mycenae   Principal city of the Akhaians; home of Agamemnon.

Nausikaa Phaiakian princess, daughter of Akinoos; she rescues Odysseus.

Neleus Father of Nestor.

Nestor Elderly king of Pylos, chief adviser of the Greeks at Troy.

Odysseus Brilliant Greek warrior and hero of *The Odyssey*.

Ogygia Island home of Kalypso.

Oidipous King of Thebes who killed his father and married his mother.

Olympos Mountain home of the gods.

Orestes Kills Klytaimnestra and Aigisthos to avenge his father's murder; foil character to Telemakhos.

Patroklos Akhilleus' best friend at Troy; his death inspires Akhilleus to fight.

Peiraios Telemakhos' trusted crewman.

Peisistratos Nestor's youngest son; he becomes a good friend of Telemakhos.

Penelope Wife of Odysseus, mother of Telemakhos.

Phaiakians Inhabitants of the island of Skheria.

Phemios Bard at the palace of Odysseus; spared in the slaughter.

Philoitios Faithful cowherd to Odysseus.

Polyphemos Another name for the Kyklopes.

Poseidon God of the sea; hostile toward Odysseus because Odysseus blinds his son, Kyklopes.

Proteus Called "the Ancient of the Sea," he has the gift of prophecy and can change his shape.

Seirenes Enchantresses who lure sailors to their death.

Skheria Island home of Alkinoos, Arete, and Nausikaa.

Styx River boundary between the land of the living and the land of the dead.

Teiresias Blind prophet met by Odysseus in the land of the dead; he foretells Odysseus' future.

Telemakhos Son of Odysseus and Penelope; secondary hero of *The Odyssey*.

Theoklymenos Traveler who accompanies Telemakhos home and interprets the omens.

Zeus King of the gods, brother of Poseidon, father of Athena; ruler on Mount Olympos.

The Critics

When the heroes who fought at Troy are described in the *Odyssey* we are clearly back in the saga world. The description of Achilles' funeral, for example, in the twenty-fourth book was very likely a commonplace of high heroic epic. But the most conspicuous theme from saga is that of Return. Nestor and Menelaos between them describe the homecoming of several of the major figures from the *Iliad*. Clearly episodes relating the return of a hero were as common as the *aristeiai* describing their triumphs in battle. The story of homecoming had a name: *nostos*. The several *nostoi* are a leitmotiv throughout the *Odyssey* which is over-all a *nostos*, being the return of Odysseus. There is a hint in the *Odyssey* that epics of *nostoi* were currently fashionable. In describing the homecoming of Agamemnon the poet lingers over details that ordinarily an epic poet takes for granted. Indeed, the occasional remark on newness and originality suggest that the particular *nostos* of Odysseus, as our poet conceived it, was perhaps not merely fashionable, but almost novel.

> *Charles Rowan Beye*, The "Iliad," The "Odyssey" and the Epic Tradition, 1966

Book XIII of the *Odyssey* describes the return of Odysseus to Ithaca; Book XVII describes his return, in disguise, to his palace, and the subsequent books describe the events leading to his return to his wife, his marriage bed, and his royal throne. Return is a fact of the *Odyssey*, a structural element in the form of the poem, but the idea of return is more than just an event of mythology, or just a consequence of the Trojan War's being fought across the Ionian sea from mainland Greece. The idea of return as a life-giving process runs deep and strong in all primitive societies, and anthropologists have often noted how totally the lives of primitive peoples are polarized around the return of natural phenomena. The eternal cycles of night and day, winter and summer, birth and death, rise and fall, permeate their lives and shape their imaginations. To secure and celebrate the return of life is often the purpose of their rituals, and the returning god, hero, or king is a feature of their myths.

> *Howard W. Clarke*, The Art of the
> "Odyssey," 1967

Before following Odysseus' travels and the further events in Ithaca, it will be useful to pause with the related questions of the method of characterization in the poem and its guiding theme. Neither question is easy, and the resonance of the myth to inwardlooking ages adds problems. Who shall catch the myriad overtones of the journey, the return, and what they jointly tell of human possibility? But a few points are clear. To Homer, unlike Dante, the journey and the return belong together. Dante's famous Ulysses of *Inferno 26* is the endless quester. His unappeased Faustian search has no place for homecoming. Because of Homer the vast world and small Ithaca both claim part of Odysseus' mind, each describes him. Unlike the homestaying suitors, he partly belongs to the world. He is seen in its varied settings, responds to them singly and, in a more important sense, cumulatively, and becomes their pupil. But though he has lived with immortals and seen the dead, none of these holds him. He refuses Calypso's offer of agelessness and immortality for mortal Penelope in Ithaca. The questions of characterization and of theme belong together because, as a character, the hero becomes known by his situations. The adventures make him; he does not in a subjective sense make the adventures.

> *M. I. Finley*, The World of Odysseus,
> 1979

Such mixed motives may seem impure or ignoble to those who take their ideals from self-sacrificing patriotism, or from self-effacing saintliness, or from self-forgetting romanticism. But these are post-Homeric concepts. Within the context of the Heroic Age and perhaps of the Homeric Age, too, this identification of one's own best interests with the general welfare of one's kith, kin, and comrades, with one's *philoi* in fact, was a saving grace for both the individual and society. All the Homeric heroes are egotists; but Odysseus' egotism has sent its roots out more widely into his personal environment than that of Agamemnon, Achilles, or Ajax.

One other aspect of Odysseus' Homeric character needs to be kept in mind at the last. In a way it is the most important of all for the development of the tradition. This is the fundamental ambiguity of his essential qualities. We have seen how prudence may decline towards timidity, tactfulness towards a blameworthy *suppressio veri*, serviceability towards servility, and so on. The ambiguity lies both in the qualities themselves and in the attitudes of others towards them. Throughout the later tradition this ambiguity in Odysseus' nature and in his reputation will vacillate between good and bad, between credit and infamy. Odysseus' personality and reputation at best are poised, as it were, on a narrow edge between Aristotelian faults of excess and deficiency. Poised between rashness and timorousness, he is prudently brave; poised between rudeness and obsequiousness he is "civilized"; poised between stupidity and overcleverness he, at his best, is wise.

William B. Stanford, "The Untypical Hero," in George Steiner and Robert Fagles, eds., Homer, A Collection of Critical Essays, *1962*